CAMBRIDGE LIBRARY COLLECTION

Books of enduring scholarly value

Naval and Military History

This series includes accounts of sea and land campaigns by eye-witnesses and contemporaries, as well as landmark studies of their social, political and economic impacts. The series focuses mainly on the period from the Renaissance to the end of the Victorian era. It includes major concentrations of material on the American and French revolutions, the British campaigns in South Asia, and nineteenth-century conflicts in Europe, such as the Peninsular and Crimean Wars. Although many of the accounts are semi-official narratives by senior officers and their relatives, the series also includes alternative viewpoints from dissenting leaders, servicemen in the lower ranks, and military wives and civilians caught up in the theatre of war.

On the Weapons, Army Organisation, and Political Maxims of the Ancient Hindus

The German Sanskrit philologist and teacher Gustav Oppert (1836–1908) worked for the greater part of his life in British India, as a professor in the Presidency College of Madras (now Chennai) and as a curator in the Government Oriental Manuscripts Library. This 1880 book considers, 'with special reference to gunpowder and firearms', the weaponry of the Hindu armies of the Middle Ages. Oppert uses two main sources, the Nitiprakasika and the Sukraniti, the former 'up to now, utterly unknown', the latter having never been 'properly described and published'. Unfortunately, the Sukraniti is now believed to be a nineteenth-century document (though drawing on older sources), and Oppert's claim that gunpowder was being used in India in the twelfth century is probably untenable. Nevertheless, the work remains an interesting study of the size, organisation and weapons of Hindu fighting forces, from bows and arrows to elephants, as well as the more anachronistic firearms.

On the Weapons, Army Organisation, and Political Maxims of the Ancient Hindus

With Special Reference to Gunpowder and Firearms

GUSTAV OPPERT

CAMBRIDGE
UNIVERSITY PRESS

CAMBRIDGE
UNIVERSITY PRESS

University Printing House, Cambridge, CB2 8BS, United Kingdom

Cambridge University Press is part of the University of Cambridge.
It furthers the University's mission by disseminating knowledge in the pursuit of education, learning and research at the highest international levels of excellence.

www.cambridge.org
Information on this title: www.cambridge.org/9781108080392

This edition first published 1880
This digitally printed version 2017

ISBN 978-1-108-08039-2 Paperback

ON THE WEAPONS, ARMY ORGANISATION, AND POLITICAL MAXIMS OF THE ANCIENT HINDUS, WITH SPECIAL REFERENCE TO GUNPOWDER AND FIREARMS.

ON THE

WEAPONS, ARMY ORGANISATION, AND POLITICAL MAXIMS

OF THE

ANCIENT HINDUS,

WITH SPECIAL REFERENCE TO GUNPOWDER AND FIREARMS.

BY

GUSTAV OPPERT, PH.D.,

PROFESSOR OF SANSKRIT, PRESIDENCY COLLEGE, MADRAS;
TELUGU TRANSLATOR TO GOVERNMENT;
CURATOR GOVERNMENT ORIENTAL MANUSCRIPTS LIBRARY;
FELLOW OF THE MADRAS UNIVERSITY, &c.

MADRAS: MESSRS. HIGGINBOTHAM & CO.
LONDON: MESSRS. TRÜBNER & CO.

1880.

MADRAS:
PRINTED BY E. KEYS, AT THE GOVERNMENT PRESS.

PREFACE.

WHILE pursuing my researches into ancient Indian history I lighted upon two ancient Sanskrit manuscripts containing interesting information on many new and important topics.

One of them, the Nītiprakāśikā, has been, I believe, up to now, utterly unknown, and the other, the Śukranīti, though known to exist, has never been properly described and published.

The Nītiprakāśikā is ascribed to Vaiśampāyana and gives among other valuable matter a full account of the Dhanurveda. It contains in fact the only accurate description which we possess of the various arms and war implements of the ancient Hindus. I esteemed it therefore proper to give as many passages as possible in full, though well aware I run the risk of tiring the reader by a long enumeration of weapons.

The chapter taken out of the Śukranīti, on the other hand, abounds with useful and interesting information, all the more worthy of being communicated, as it enters into subjects connected with war and politics from a truly Indian standpoint, which may perhaps command additional attention now that a war is being waged within the north-western boundaries of ancient India.

The organisation of the ancient Indian armies is well and clearly described in its outlines ; the division of the army into a veteran reserve and young line-troops is remarkable. The same can be said of the laws according to which war ought to be conducted. The maxims of the Dharmayuddha recall to our memory the laws of chivalry existing during the Middle-ages, and the former like the latter seem only to have been followed when it appeared convenient to do so; for some of the most renowned Indian heroes, as Rāma and Kṛṣṇa, are credited with having stooped at times to mean and treacherous acts, in order to gain victory. In recent times we have witnessed a revival of this humane feeling, in the outcry which was raised against explosive bullets and in the Geneva Convention, which was instituted to mitigate the horrors of war.

It is of peculiar interest that the statements found in these two ancient works tally with the few remarks on Indian army organisation which we glean from the fragments of ancient Greek and Roman writers.

The Nītiprakāśikā and the Śukranīti, while testifying to a high civilisation prevailing in ancient India, cast also some light on the recension of such works as the Mahābhārata and the Mānavadharmaśāstra.

The difficult and intricate question about the ancient home of gunpowder and firearms, I trust to have finally settled.

I may close with the remark that this book should only be considered as an occasional offshoot of my studies in Indian history, and as nothing more.

GUSTAV OPPERT.

MADRAS, 23*rd August* 1880.

CONTENTS.

ON THE WEAPONS, ARMY ORGANISATION AND POLITICAL MAXIMS OF THE ANCIENT HINDUS, WITH SPECIAL REFERENCE TO GUNPOWDER AND FIREARMS

CHAPTER I.

ON THE WEAPONS AND WAR IMPLEMENTS OF THE ANCIENT HINDUS.

Our knowledge of the history of the ancient Hindus is very limited, and there is not much hope of our becoming better informed, as the most important factor for providing such knowledge, *i.e.*, a historical literature or a sufficient number of authentic records is not existing in India, in fact seems never to have existed. While we possess ample material to reconstruct to some extent the history of the ancient Egyptians, Assyrians, Hebrews, Persians or Greeks, the Hindus have left us no sufficiently trustworthy records of the past, to enable us to do the same with respect to Indian history, that has been done to the history of other ancient nations.

The combined influences of climate, geographical position, political circumstances, education, religious belief, and habit have conspired to destroy any taste for historical researches, even if such had existed formerly. Internecine wars, all the more cruelly conducted, as they severed the links of previous relationship and friendship, either undertaken for the sake of political or religious supremacy, and continual invasions of foreigners unsettling entirely all domestic affairs and civic arrangements could not excite so great an interest as to be remembered with care and committed to posterity by recording them. Nobody likes to remember saddening occurrences, and a few bright spots excepted, the political history of India reveals one of the most dismal pictures of human existence.

Moreover the exalted position in the social ladder which a Brahman occupies in his own estimation, does not induce him to interest himself in the worldly fate of others. Every Brahman regards himself as a descendant of one of the great divine sages, and obtains, if pious, final beatitude through this descent. To ensure it he has to remember and to revere the memory of his three immediate predecessors—father, grandfather, and great-grandfather; and, as every previous ancestor has observed the same practice, he is in his mind certain of his ultimate prosperity. Why should he, therefore, engage himself in the investigation of a subject in which he is not interested and which can confer on him no benefit?

The subject of Indian history is a very difficult one, not only from the absence of trustworthy ancient records, but also from the necessity—and in this respect it resembles all Asiatic history—that the historian should be an Orientalist. Historical science is strictly allied to, and dependent on, philological science, and without a knowledge of the mother tongue of a nation, or, at all events of the languages in which the original and most important sources of its history are recorded, no person is competent to undertake to write the history of a nation, for, being unable to read the original records himself, first, he is not able to judge them critically; and, secondly, it is beyond his power to detect any mistakes made by translators. Were all reports true and all translations correct, the drudgery and anxiety of a historian would be considerably reduced, but reports and translations which fulfil these requirements are still a *desideratum*.[1]

The two great epics and the purānas are the works which mainly represent the historical branch of Indian literature. But woe betide him who would look up to them as authentic and trustworthy sources. However important and interesting in many other respects, historical accuracy is not a quality they aim at; for they are rather a depository of legendary myths, which are enlarged by an imagination morbidly fond of wonders. Nevertheless they must not be quite thrown away as useless, for they may contain here and there some grains of historical truth, as a rock may contain some dispersed grains of gold, though they can with difficulty only be separated from their less precious surroundings. Besides the epics and purānas, the law books make sometimes occasional remarks which throw light on historical subjects; they together with the works on polity allow us merely an insight into the manners and customs of the old Hindus; and in this respect they are of the highest importance. In the following pages we shall discuss the customs of the ancient Indians so far as they bear on the nature of their arms. Two ancient Sanskrit works, the Nītiprakāśikā of Vaiśampāyana and the Śukranīti of Uśanas or Śukrācārya, are in my possession which contain important, and up to the present generally unknown information on this subject, which I hope will be of interest to the reader.

---

[1] Yet in this time of literary upholstery people desirous of gaining literary success often overlook these facts so evident to all outsiders. A sad example of labor thus thrown away and of much patient research so fruitlessly spent, is the voluminous history of the Mongols, in the preface of the first volume of which the author, Mr. Henry H. Howorth, says that he approaches 'the problem as an ethnologist and historian and not as a linguist,' and that he had 'no access to the authorities in their original language, and only to translations and commentaries.' This confession, however honest, need not have been made, as the work itself throughout suggests by its defects the want of linguistic attainments which for a writer on oriental history is a *conditio sine quâ non*.

The Nītiprakāśikā is an extract from a larger work devoted to the Nītiśāstra,[2] which is ascribed to Vaiśampāyana, the same to whom the Yajurveda is assigned, and who recited the contents of the Mahābhārata to Janamejaya, the great-grandson of Arjuna, the son of Pāṇḍu. Vaiśampāyana is introduced in the Nītiprakāśikā as communicating at Takṣaśilā in the Panjab to the same king Janamejaya the nature of the Dhanurveda, the peculiarity of the weapons and of all the matter connected with war and the administration of the kingdom. The Nītiprakāśikā is divided into eight books, the first five speak about the Dhanurveda and weapons in general, the sixth and seventh contain remarks on the divisions and constitution of an army, and the eighth on different subjects connected with the royal prerogative and the duties of subjects.

Horace Hayman Wilson, the eminent Sanskrit scholar, has devoted a special article to " the art of war as known to the Hindus ;" but this excellent essay was written many years ago and does not enter deeply into the question of gunpowder and firearms, which is particularly commented upon in the following lines.

The smallest unit of the Indian army, a *patti*, is described to consist of 1 chariot, 1 elephant, 3 horses, and 5 men. The *Senāmukha*, *Gulma*, *Gaṇa*, *Vāhinī*, *Pṛtanā*, *Camū*, and *Anīkinī* are respectively three times as big as the corps preceding them, and the 9th formation, which was called *Akṣauhiṇī* and was considered to represent a complete army, was ten times as numerous as the preceding Anīkinī.[3] The Nītiprakāśikā, after describing the original patti, goes on to say that a chariot has a retinue of 10 elephants, 100 horses, and 1,000 men ;

[2] I hope soon to obtain a copy of this work, as it is in the library of one of my native friends. It is perhaps the work alluded to in the following words contained in the Āśvalāyana Gṛhya : " Sumantu-Jaimini-Vaiśampāyana-Paila-sūtrabhāshya-bhārata-mahābhārata-dharmacāryāḥ."

[3] Amarakośa, II, viii, 48 and 49 ; Nītiprakāśikā, vii, 5. " Eko ratho gajaścaiko narāḥ pañca hayāḥ trayaḥ."

an elephant one of 100 horses and 1,000 men; a horse one of 1,000 soldiers, and that a foot soldier had ten followers.[4]

According to the first mentioned scale the different corps would have the following strength :—

Army Corps.	Chariot.	Elephant.	Horse.	Foot.
Patti	1	1	3	5
Senāmukha	3	3	9	15
Gulma	9	9	27	45
Gaṇa	27	27	81	135
Vāhinī	81	81	243	405
Pṛtanā	243	243	729	1,215
Camū	729	729	2,187	3,645
Anīkinī	2,187	2,187	6,561	10,935
Akṣauhiṇī	21,870	21,870	65,610	109,350

According to the second estimate one chariot alone demands an extraordinary number of supporters. And indeed the Nītiprakāśikā lays down that the various army corps should have the following constitution[5] :—

Army Corps.	Chariot.	Elephant.	Horse.	Foot.
Patti	1	10	1,000	100,000
Senāmukha	3	30	3,000	300,000
Gulma	9	90	9,000	900,000
Gaṇa	27	270	27,000	2,700,000
Vāhinī	81	810	81,000	8,100,000
Pṛtanā	243	2,430	243,000	24,300,000
Camū	729	7,290	729,000	72,900,000
Anīkinī	2,187	21,870	2,187,000	218,700,000
Akṣauhiṇī	21,870	218,700	21,870,000	2,187,000,000

[4] Nītiprakāśikā vii, 6–8.

6. Nāgā daśa rathasyāsya śatam aśvāssahānugāḥ
sahasram tu narāḥ proktāḥ parivārā nṛpājñayā.

7. Ekasyaikasya nāgasya śatam aśvāḥ prayāyinaḥ
padātayaḥ sahasram tu pratyaṅgeśvanuyāyinaḥ.

8. Ekasyaikasya cāśvasya sahasram tu padātayaḥ
daśa caitān pattīn yuṅktvā kārtsnena gaṇanā tviyam.

[5] Nītiprakāśikā, vii, 9–11, 27–30.

9. Eko ratho daśa gajāḥ sahasram cātra vājinaḥ
lakṣasaṅkhyā narāḥ pattāvevam agre'pi yojanā.

The Hindu delights in large numbers, and to this propensity must be ascribed this exorbitant calculation. The population of the whole earth is generally assumed to amount to 1,075,000,000 souls, and in the Nītiprakāśikā we are told that a complete army requires a number of men, which surpasses by more than a half the number of all the inhabitants of this globe.

The Śukranīti gives a much more sensible distribution. According to that work the aggregate of the military unit would be 5 chariots, 10 elephants, 40 camels, 64 bulls, 320 horses, and 1,280 men.[6]

The formation of an army into different columns is a subject to which great attention was paid. Four different kinds of such columns or *vyūhas* are enumerated—the *Daṇḍa*, *Bhoga*, *Asaṁhata*, and *Maṇḍala*; the first had 17 varieties, the second 5, the third 6, and the fourth 2. Besides these, five most important columns were not enrolled in any of these four sets; they were called *Varāha*, *Makara*, *Garuḍa*, *Krauñca*, and *Padma*.[7]

---

10. Pratyaṅgaistriguṇaiḥ sarvaiḥ kramāt ākhyā yathottaram
anīkinīm daśaguṇām āhurakṣauhiṇīm budhaḥ.
11. Senāmukhe tu guṇitāḥ trayaścaiva rathā gajāḥ
triṁśaṭ trilakṣapadatāḥ trisahasram hi vājinaḥ; &c., &c.
27. Akṣauhiṇyām tvekaviṁśatsahasrāṇi janādhipa
tathā cāṣṭaśatam caiva saptatim rathagām viduḥ.
28. Aṣṭādaśasahasrāṇi dve lakṣe ca nareśvara
tathā saptaśatam caiva gajānām gaṇanā tviyam.
29. Dve koṭī caiva lakṣāṇām aṣṭādaśa mahīpate
tathā saptatisahasrā gandharvāśśīghrayāyinaḥ.
30. Dve cārbude ca koṭiścāpyaṣṭādaśasamīritāḥ
lakṣāṇām saptatiścaiva padātīnām itīyatī.

[6] *See* Śukranīti, Chapter V, ślokas 20, 21.

[7] *See* Nītiprakāśikā, vi, 3–9.

3. Daṇḍo bhogo'saṁhataśca maṇḍalavyūha eva ca
vyūhāścatvāra evaite teṣu bhedān bravīmyaham.
4. Pradaro dṛḍhakassatyaścāpabhūsvakṣireva ca
supratiṣṭho'pratiṣthaśca śyeno vijayasañjayau.

All these troops were commanded by generals, whose rank depended upon the number of troops under their orders. The ministers of the king held mostly also the office of generals.

All the soldiers, from the private to the commander-in-chief, received their pay regularly every month. The crown-prince, who was generally the next in command to the king, received every month 5,000 *varvas*, or gold coins ;[8] the commander-in-chief drew 4,000 varvas; the atiratha, the first charioteer, who was usually a royal prince, received 3,000 varvas; the mahāratha 2,000 varvas; the rathika and the gajayodhi, 1,000 varvas each; the ardharatha 500 varvas; the ekaratha (commander of a chariot), and the leader of an elephant got each 300 niṣkas. The general commanding all the cavalry obtained 3,000 niṣkas; the general in command of the whole infantry received 2,000 niṣkas. An officer commanding 1,000 men of infantry got 500 niṣkas; an officer who led the same number of troopers received 1,000 niṣkas;

---

5. Viśālovijayaḥ sūcī sthūṇo karṇaścamūmukhaḥ
 mukhāsyovijayaśceti daṇḍasaptadaśātmakaḥ.
6. Gomūtrikā haṁsikā ca sañcārī śakaṭastathā
 evam karapatantīti bhogabhedāstu pañca vai.
7. Ardhacandrakaṭaddhāro vajraśśakaṭakastathā
 śṛṅgī ca kākapādīca godhiketyaparasmṛtaḥ.
8. Asaṁhataḥ ṣaḍvidhassyāt ityāhurvyūhakovidāḥ
 sarvabhadro durjayaśca maṇḍalopi dvidhā iti.
9. Vārāhī makaravyūho gāruḍaḥ krauñca eva ca
 padmādyāścaṅgavaikalyāt etebhyaste pṛthak smṛtāh.

[8] The value of the varva, which is an ancient coin, is difficult to determine. In the Nītiprakāśikā, VI, 89–101, the rewards which are to be given to soldiers who kill a king, a crown-prince, a commander-in-chief, a leader of an Akṣauhiṇī, a councillor, and a minister, &c., &c., are also fixed in varvas.

89. Dadyāt prahṛṣṭo niyutam varvāṇām rājaghātine
 tadardhantatsutavadhe senāpativadhe tathā.
90. Akṣauhiṇīpativadhe tadardham paricakṣate
 mantryamātyavadhe caiva tadardham tu pradāpayet, &c., &c.

Śloka 89 is also found in the Kāmandakīya, XIX, 18, having been most probably taken from this work of Vaiśampāyana.

an officer who had 100 small pattis under his command and who must ride on a horse drew only 7 varvas, while a private got 5 suvarṇas.

The following fourteen persons got only each 15 varvas a month :—1, an elephant driver ; 2, a charioteer ; 3, an ensign-bearer ; 4, a superintendent of wheels ; 5, an officer in command of 300 men of infantry ; 6, a camel-express ; 7, a messenger ; 8, the head gate-keeper ; 9, the chief-bard ; 10, the chief-singer ; 11, the chief panegyrist ; 12, the head store-keeper ; 13, the army paymaster, and 14, the muster master.[9] The Śukranīti contains another scale of salaries.[10] If this scale of salaries is correct and if the salaries were really paid, one would feel inclined to think, that an extensive gold currency existed in ancient India.

Armour was worn by the warriors, and even elephants and horses were similarly protected.

The description of the weapons which follows in this chapter is mainly taken from the Nītiprakāśikā.

---

[9] *See* Nītiprakāśikā, VII, 33-42.

33. Yuvarājāya varvāṇām pañcasāhasrakī bhṛtiḥ
sarvasenāpraṇetre ca catussāhasrakī ca sā.

34. Bhṛtiścatirathe deyā varvāṇām trisahasrakam
mahārathāya sahasradvayam rājñādhimāsakam.

35. Vetanam rathikāyātha sāhasram gajayodhine
dadyāt ardharathāyātha vetanam śatapañcakam.

36. Ekasmai rathikāyātha tādṛśe gajasādine
niṣkāṇām triśatam dadyāt yatastau tatkuṭumbiṇau.

37. Sarvāśvādhipatī rājñastrisahasram sa cārhati
pādātādhipatiścāpi dvisahasrasya bhājanam.

38. Pādātānām sahasrasya netre pañcaśatam smṛtam
tathā caśvasahasreśe sahasram vetanam bhavet.

39. Śatapattyadhipe sapta varvāṇām hayayāyine
padātaye suvarṇānām pañcakam vetanam bhavet.

40. Gajayantussaratheśca dhvajine cakrapāya ca
padātitriśateśāya pathikoṣṭracarāya ca.

41. Vārttikādhipateścāpi vetriṇām pataye tathā
sūtamāgadhavandīnām pataye vīvadhādhipe.

42. Senāyā bhṛtidhātre ca bhaṭānām gaṇanāpare
māsi māsi tu varvāṇām daśapañca ca vetanam.

[10] *See* Śukranīti, Chapter V, śl. 23-28.

The Hindu is fond of connecting everything, even the most material substance, with some metaphysical cause. We must not be surprised, therefore, if weapons and arms do not make an exception to this rule.

A supernatural origin is ascribed to all armour. The primeval Dakṣa had two daughters—Jayā and Suprabhā—who were given in marriage to Kṛśāśva, the mind-begotten son of Brahma. Jayā became, according to a promise of Brahma, the mother of all weapons and missiles, while her sister Suprabhā brought forth at first ten sons who were called Saṁhāras *restraining spells;* and afterwards through the special favor of Brahma an eleventh son, Sarvamocana (releaser of all), was born.[11]

The knowledge of everything connected with weapons and arms is confined to the Dhanurveda, *i.e.*, the knowledge of the bow, and he only, who is well acquainted with this Veda, can hope to conquer his foes. The Dhanurveda is one of the four Upavedas. Even the gods had originally no intimate acquaintance with the precepts of the Dhanurveda, and this deficiency was one of the causes why they were at one time totally defeated by the demons or asuras. Eventually the gods were instructed in the mysteries of the Dhanurveda; and this Veda was communicated to Pṛthu by Brahma himself.

The Dhanurveda when personified is credited with possessing four feet, eight arms, and three eyes, and Sāṅkhyāyana is mentioned as the head of his Gotra or race. In his four arms on the right he holds a thunderbolt (*vajra*),

---

[11] *See* Nītiprakāśikā, 1, 45–47 ; II, 38.

45. Kṛśāśvo mānasaḥ putro dve jāye tasya sammate
jayā ca suprabhā caiva dakṣakanye mahāmatī.

46. Jayā labdhavarā matto (*a*) śastrāṇyastrāṇyasūta vai
paścāt daśa parā cāpi tāvat putrān ajījanat.

47. Saṁhārān nāmadurdharṣān durākrāmān balīyasaḥ
mantradaivatasaṁyogāt śāstrāṇyastratvam āpnuvan.

38. Sarvamocananāmā tu suprabhātanayo mahān
muktāmuktākhilaśamo madvarāt (*a*) prathitaḥ paraḥ.

(*a*) Brahma speaks here himself.

a sword (*khaḍga*), a bow (*dhanu*), and a discus (*cakra*) ; in his four arms on the left are a hundred-killer (*śataghnī*), a club (*gadā*), a spear (*śūla*), and a battle axe (*paṭṭiśa*). His crest is provided with charms; his body is polity; his armour is a spell; his heart represents withdrawing spells; his two earrings are the weapons and missiles; his ornaments are the various war movements ; his eyes are yellow; he is girt with the garland of victory, and he rides on a bull.[12]

The spell which effects the destruction of one's enemies and which grants victory is as follows: *Om namo bhagavate dham dhanurvedāya mām rakṣa rakṣa mama śatrūn bhakṣaya bhakṣaya hum paṭ svā hā* ; *i.e.*, "Om salutation to the dham dhanurveda, protect, protect me, devour, devour my enemies hum paṭ svā hā." If these 32 syllables are 32,000 times repeated the supplication will be successful.[13]

The arms are divided, according to their nature, into *mukta* or those which are thrown, *amukta* or those which are not thrown, *muktāmukta* or those which are either thrown or not thrown, and into *mantramukta* or those which are thrown by

---

[12] *See* Nītiprakāśikā, II, 1–4.

1. Catuṣpācca dhanurvedo raktavarṇaścaturmukhaḥ
aṣṭabāhustrinetraśca sāṅkhyāyanasagotravān.
2. Vajram khaḍgo dhanuścakram dakṣabāhucatuṣṭaye
śataghnīca gadāśūlapaṭṭiśā vāmabāhuṣu.
3. Prayogakoṭīrayuto nītyaṅgo mantrakañcukaḥ
upasaṁhārahṛdayaśśastrāstrobhayakuṇḍalaḥ.
4. Anekavalgitākārabhūṣaṇaḥ piṅgalekṣaṇaḥ
jayamālāparivṛto vṛṣārūḍassa ucyate.

[13] *See* Ibidem, II, 5-9.

5. Etammantram pravakṣyāmi vairijālanikṛntanam
ātmasainyasvapakṣāṇām ātmanaścābhirakṣakam.
6. Ādau praṇavam uccārya na ma ityakṣare tataḥ
vateti bhagapūrvam dham dhanurvedāya coccaret.
7. Mām rakṣa rakṣetyuccārya mama śatrūn atho vadet
bhakṣayeti dviruccārya hum paṭ svā hetyathoccaret.
8. Aham evam ṛṣiścāsya gāyatrī chanda ucyate
maheśvaro devatāsya viniyogo'rinigrahe.
9. Dvātriṁśadvarṇakamanum varṇasaṅkhyāsahasrakaiḥ
japitvā siddhim āpnoti ripūṅścāpyadhitiṣṭhati.

The expression *dham dhanurveda* is formed in the same way as *Ram Rāma*, *Vim Vijñeśvara*, &c.

spells.[14] This classification is more theoretical than practical, as it is not strictly followed. The gods can, moreover through the application of spells, turn all weapons into projectiles.[15]

The Agnipurāṇa arranges the weapons in five classes, into 1, those thrown by machines, *yantramukta;* 2, those thrown by the hand, *pāṇimukta ;* 3, those thrown and drawn back, *muktasandhārita ;* 4, those which are not thrown, *amukta ;* and, 5, the weapons which the body provides for the personal struggle, the *bāhuyuddha.*[16] Other classifications besides these exist, but the difference between them is not essential.

Twelve projectiles and projectile weapons constitute the division of the *mukta* or thrown weapons.

1. The *dhanu* (bow) is personified as a being which has a broad neck, a small face, a slender waist, and a strong back. He is four cubits in height, and bent in three places. He has a long tongue, and his mouth has terrible tusks ; his color is that of blood, and he makes always a gurgling noise. He is covered with garlands of entrails, and licks continually with his tongue the two corners of his mouth.[17]

According to the rules laid down in the Dhanurveda the bow should be bent by the left hand, the bowstring should be taken by the right hand, and the arrow be placed on the

---

[14] *See* Ibidem, II, 11–13.

11. Muktam caivā hyamuktam ca muktāmuktam ataḥ param
mantramuktam ca catvāri dhanurvedapadāni vai.
12. Muktam baṇādi vijñeyam khaḍgādikam amuktakam
sōpasaṁhāram astram tu muktāmuktam udāharet.
13. Upasaṁhārarahitam mantram uktam ihocyate
caturbhirebhiḥ pādaistu dhanurvedaḥ prakāśate.

[15] *See* Ibidem I. 47 b, note 11.

[16] *See* Agnipurāṇa (Dhanurveda) 148, 2.
Yantramuktam pāṇimuktam muktasandhāritam tathā
amuktam bāhuyuddham ca pañcadhā tat prakīrttitam.

[17] *See* Nītiprakāśikā, II, 17 ; and IV. 8, 9.

8. Pṛthugrīvam sūkṣmaśiraḥ tanumadhyam supṛṣṭhavat
catuṣkiṣkuprāṁśudeham triṇatam dīrghajihvakam.
9. Daṁṣṭrākarālavadanam raktābham ghargharasvanam
āntramālāparikṣiptam lelihānam ca sṛkvaṇī.

thumb and between the fingers of the bowhand on the back of the bow.[18]

The length of the bow, and consequently also of the arrow, varies. Two strings are generally fixed to a bow, and the archer wears on his left arm a leather protection against the bowstring, and a quiver on his back. Those well skilled in archery distinguish fourteen different movements which can be made when using the bow. In the Agnipurāṇa the bow is declared to be the best weapon.

In the law book of Manu we read, that one bowman placed on a wall can fight a hundred men, and that a hundred archers can fight ten thousand; therefore a fort is recommended. In the Śukranīti occurs the same verse but instead of the word for bow *dhanu* that for a missile *astra* is given, which imparts a wider meaning to the sentence, especially if it is taken to allude to firearms, unless *dhanu* itself stands for missile in general.[19]

---

[18] Ibidem, II, 17; and IV, 11–14.

11. Dhanurvedavidhānena nāmya vāmakareṇa tat
dakṣiṇena jyayā yojya pṛṣṭhe madhye pragṛhya tat.
12. Vāmāṅguṣṭham tadudare pṛṣṭhe tu caturaṅgulīḥ
puṅkhamadhye jyayā yojya svāṅgulīvivareṇa tu.
13. Ākarṇam tu samākṛṣya dṛṣṭim lakṣye viveśya ca
lakṣyāt anyad apaśyanstu kṛtapuṅkhaḥ prayogavit.
14. Yadā muñcet śaram vidhye kṛtahastastadocyate
evam bāṇāḥ prayoktavyāḥ hyātmārakṣyaḥ prayatnataḥ.

[19] *See* Nītiprakāśikā, II, 17, and IV, 18–20.

18 Lakṣyasya pratisandhānam ākarṣaṇavikarṣaṇe
paryākarṣānukarṣauca maṇḍalīkaraṇam tathā.
19 Pūraṇam sthāraṇam caiva dhūnanam bhrāmaṇam tathā
āsannadūrapātauca pṛṣṭhamadhyamapātane.
20 Etāni valgitānyāhuścaturdaśadhanurvidaḥ.

Compare Śukranīti, Chapter V, śl. 152; Agnipurāṇa, 148, 6–37; 149, 1–19.

See Manu, VII, 74, (Hitopadeśa, III, 50 Pañcatantra, I, 252).

74. Ekaḥ śatam yodhayati prākārastho dhānurdharaḥ.
śatam daśa sahasrāṇi tasmāt durgam viśiṣyate.

and compare these verses with Śukranīti, IV, VI, 10.

10. Ekaḥ śatam yodhayati durgastho'stradharo yadī
śatam daśasahasrāṇi tasmāt durgam samāśrayet.

2. The *iṣu* (arrow) has a dark large body; is three cubits long, an añjali (*i.e.*, the hollow of the two hands) in circumference and goes very far; two movements are ascribed to the arrow.[20]

3. The *bhiṇḍivāla* or *bhiṇḍipāla* (crooked club) has a crooked body: its head, which is bent and broad, is a cubit long, and it is a hand in circumference. It is first whirled thrice and then thrown against the foot of the enemy. When throwing the bhiṇḍivāla, the left foot should be placed in front.[21]

4. The *śakti* (spear) is represented as being two cubits long, with a steady sideway movement. It has a sharp tongue, a horrible claw, and makes a sound like a bell. It has an open mouth, is very dark, and is colored with the blood of the enemy. It is covered with garlands of entrails; has the mouth of a lion, and is fearful to look at. It is as broad as a fist and goes very far. It must be taken up and thrown with two hands. Its movements are of six kinds.[22]

---

[20] *See* Ibidem, I, 17; and IV, 28, 29.

28. Iṣurnīlabṛhaddeho dvihastotsedhasaṁyutaḥ
paridhyā cāñjalimito'nalpamātragatistu saḥ.

29. Bhrāmaṇam kṣepaṇam ceti dve gatī sthūlasannate.

Compare Śukranīti, Chapter V, śl. 152.

[21] *See* Ibidem, I, 17, and IV, 30, 31.

30. Bhiṇḍivālastu vakrāṅgo namraśīrṣo bṛhacchirāḥ
hastamātrotsedhayuktaḥ karasammitamaṇḍalaḥ

31. Tribhrāmaṇam visargaśca vāmapādapurassaran
pādaghātāt ripuhaṇo dhāryaḥ pādātamaṇḍalaiḥ.

Compare Agnipurāṇa, 151, 15-

[22] *See* Ibidem, I, 17, and IV, 32–35.

32. Śaktirhastadvayotsedhā tiryaggatiranākulā
tīkṣṇajihvogranakharā ghaṇṭānādabhayaṅkarī.

33. Vyāditāsyātinīlāca śatruśoṇitarañjitā
āntramālāparikṣiptā siṁhāsyā ghoradarśanā.

34. Bṛhatsarurdūragamā parvatendravidāriṇī
bhujadvayapreraṇīyā yuddhe jayavidhāyinī.

35. Tolanam bhrāmaṇam caiva valganam nāmanam tathā
mocanam bhedanam ceti ṣaṇmārgāśśāktisaṁśritāḥ.

5. The *drughaṇa* (hatchet) has an iron body, a crooked neck, and a broad head. It is 50 aṅgulas long and a fist in circumference. Four movements are peculiar to it.[23]

6. The *tomara* (tomahawk) has a wooden body and a metal head formed like a bunch of flowers. It is three cubits long, has a red color, and is not crooked. It is moved in three ways.[24]

7. The *nalikā* (musket) has a straight body, is thin-limbed, and hollow in the middle. It pierces the vital parts, is dark, and discharges the missiles of the Droṇicāpa. When it is to be used, it is taken up, ignited, and pierces the mark. These are the three actions connected with the nalikā.

It seems to have been a small-sized gun, a sort of carbine, as it is only described as effective against enemies standing near.[25]

8. The *laguḍa* (club) is described as having a small foot, a broad shoulder, and a broad head. The foot part is surrounded with metal. It is small and very broad. It has the

---

[23] Ibidem, II. 17 ; IV. 36, 37.

36. Drughaṇastvāyassāṅgassyāt vakragrīvo bṛhacchiraḥ
pañcāśat aṅgulyutsedho muṣṭisammitamaṇḍalaḥ.

37. Unnāmanam prapātam ca sphoṭanam dāraṇam tathā
catvāryetāni drughaṇe valgitāni śritāni vai.

[24] Ibidem, II. 17 ; IV. 38, 39.

38. Tomaraḥ kāṣṭhakāyassyāt lohaśīrṣaḥ sugucchavān
hastatrayonnatāṅgaśca raktavarṇastvavakragaḥ.

39. Uddhānam vinivṛttiśca vedhanam ceti tattrikam
valgitam śastratattvajñāḥ kathayanti narādhipāḥ.

Compare Agnipurāṇa, 151, 10.

[25] Ibidem, II. 17 ; IV. 40, 41.

40. Nalikā ṛjudehā syāt tanvaṅgī madhyarandhrikā
marmacchedakarī nīlā droṇicāpaśareriṇī.

41. Grahaṇam dhmāpanam caiva syūtam ceti gatitrayam
tām āśritam viditvā tu jetāsannān ripūn yudhi.

Mallinātha uses the expression *droṇicāpa* in his commentary to Naiṣadha, II, 28. *Compare* p. 68.

shape of a tooth. It has a hard body and is two cubits high. Its movements are of four kinds.[26]

9. The *pāśa* (lasso) is composed of very small scales, made of metal. It has a triangular form, is one span in circumference, and is ornamented with leaden balls. It has three peculiar movements of its own. According to the Agnipurāna it is 10 cubits long, round, and the noose is a hand in circumference. It is not regarded as a noble weapon.[27]

10. The *cakra* (discus) has the form of a circular disk with a quadrangular hole in its midst. Its color is like that of indigo water and its circumference amounts to two spans or 10 cubits according to the Śukranīti. Five or seven motions are connected with the discus practice. It is most probably identical with the quoit still in use in some Sikh regiments and also among the troops of Native Indian princes.[28]

11. The *dantakaṇṭaka* (tooth-thorn) is a thorn made of metal, is broad at the front, has a thin tail, and its color resembles charcoal. It is an arm high, has a good handle, is straight in

---

[26] *See* Ibidem, II. 17 ; IV. 42, 43.

42. Laguḍassūkṣmapādassyāt pṛthvaṁśaḥ sthūlaśīrṣakaḥ
lohabaddhāgrabhāgaśca hrasvadehassupīvaraḥ.

43. Dantakāyo dṛḍhāṅgaśca tathā hastadvayonnataḥ
utthānam patanam caiva peṣaṇam pothanam tathā.

Compare Agnipurāṇa, 151, 15.

[27] *See* Ibidem, II. 17 ; IV. 45, 46.

45. Pāśassusūkṣmāvayavo lohadhātustrikoṇavān
prādeśaparidhissīsagulikābharaṇāñcitaḥ.

46. Prasāraṇam veṣṭanam ca kartanam ceti te trayaḥ
yogāḥ pāśāśritā loke pāśāḥ kṣudrasamāśritāḥ.

Compare Agnipurāṇa, 150, 2–6 ; 151, 6, 7.

[28] *See* Ibidem II. 17 ; IV. 47, 48.

47. Cakram tu kuṇḍalākāram ante svaśrasamanvitam
nīlīsalilavarṇam tat prādeśadvayamaṇḍalam.

48. Granthanam bhrāmaṇam caiva kṣepaṇam parikartanam
dalanam ceti pañcaiva gatayaścakrasaṁśritāḥ.

Compare Śukranīti, Chapter V, śl. 156 ; Agnipurāṇa, 151, 8.

its body, and looks frightful. Two movements are required for using it.[29]

12. The *musuṇḍi* (octagonheaded club) has broad knots, a broad body, and a good handle for the fist. It is three arms long, and has the fearful color of a cobra. Its two principal movements are the jerking and the whirling.[30]

B. The class of the *amukta* weapons includes twenty different species.

1. The *vajra* (thunderbolt) was, according to tradition, made out of the backbone of the sage Dadhīci. It keeps its mythical character throughout. Nothing can withstand its splendour, and it was originally made for the destruction of the demon Vṛtra. It shines brightly with the light of a krore of suns, and it resembles the fire which shone at the dissolution of the world. Its fangs extend to a yojana (10 miles) in length, and its tongue too is most horrible. It resembles the night of destruction at the end of the world, and is covered with 100 knots. Its breadth amounts to five yojanas and its length to 10 yojanas. Its periphery is covered with sharp points ; in color it resembles lightning ; a broad strong handle is fixed to it. Its movements are four in number.[31]

---

[29] *See* Ibidem, II. 17 ; IV. 49, 50.

49. Dantakaṇṭakanāmā tu lohakaṇṭakadehavān
agre pṛthussūkṣmapucchaścāṅgārasanibhākṛtiḥ.

50. Bāhūnnatassutsaruśca daṇḍakāyo'gralocanaḥ
pātanam granthanam ceti dve gatī dantakaṇṭake.

[30] *See* Ibidem II. 18 ; IV. 51, 52.

51. Musuṇḍī tu bṛhadgranthirbṛhaddehassusatsaruḥ
bāhutrayasamutsedhaḥ kṛṣṇasarpogravarṇavān.

52. Yāpanam ghūrṇanam ceti dve gatī tat samāśrite.

Another form of the word is bṛsuṇḍı.

[31] *See* Ibidem, II. 19 ; V. 1–6.

1. Amuktaprathamam vajram vakṣyāmi tava tacchṛṇu
aprameyabalam vajram kāmarūpadharam ca tat.

2. Dadhīcipṛṣṭhāsthijanyam sarvatejaḥ praśāmakam
vṛtrāsuranipātārtham daivatejopavṛṁhitam.

2. The *ilī* (hand-sword) is two cubits long, has no hilt for the protection of the hand, and is black colored. The front part of the blade is curved, and it is five fingers broad. Four movements are peculiar to it.[32]

3. The *paraśu* (axe) is a thin stick with a broad mouth. Its face is in front, curved like a half moon, the body is dirty colored, but the face is shining. At the foot end is the handle, and it has a head. Its height is the length of an arm. Its qualities are felling and splitting.[33]

4. The *gośīrṣa* (cow-horn spear) is two feet long; it is wooden in the lower parts and iron on the upper part. It has a blade, is of dark metal color, is three-cornered and has a good handle. Its height amounts to 16 thumbs; it is sharp in front and broad in the middle. Indra presented the gośīrṣa together with a seal to Manu, and the cow-horn spear and the signet-ring became henceforth the emblems of royalty. The gośīrṣa is handled with four movements.[34]

5. The *asidhenu* (stiletto) is one cubit long, has no hand-guard at the handle, is dark colored, has three edges, is two

---

3. Koṭisūryapratīkāśam pralayānalasannibham
yojanotsedhadaṁṣṭrābhirjihvayā cātighorayā.
4. Kālarātrinikāśam tat śataparvasamāvṛtam
pañcayojanavistāram unnatam daśayojanam.
5. Apimaṇḍalasaṁvītam paritaḥ tīkṣṇakoṭimat
taṭidgauram ca pṛthunā tsaruṇā ca virājitam.
6. Cālanam dhūnanam caiva chedanam bhedanam tathā
valgitāni ca catvāri sadā vajram śritāni vai.
Compare Agnipurāṇa, 151, 16.

[32] Ibidem, II. 19; V. 7, 8.
7. Īlī hastadvayotsedhā karatrarahitatsaruḥ
śyāmā bhugnāgraphalakā pañcāṅgulisuvistṛtā.
8. Sampātam samudīrṇam ca nigrahapragrahau tathā
ilīm etāni catvāri valgitāni śritāni vai.

[33] Ibidem, II. 19; V. 9, 10.
9. Paraśussūkṣmayaṣṭissyāt viśālāsyaḥ puromukhaḥ
ardhacandrāgre koṭistu malināṅgassphuranmukhaḥ.
10. Tsarupādassaśikharo bāhumātronnatākṛtiḥ
pātanam chedanam ceti guṇau paraśum āśritau.
Compare Agnipurāṇa, 151, 13.

[34] Ibidem, II. 19; V. 11–14.
11. Gośīrṣam gośiraḥ prakhyam prasāritapadadvayam
adhastāt dāruyantrādyam ūrdhvāyaḥphalakāñcitam.

thumbs broad, and is applicable for fighting at near quarters It is fastened with a waistbelt and is called the sister of the sword. It requires three movements. It is worn by kings.[35]

6. The *lavitra* (scythe) has a crooked shape, is broad at the back and sharp in front. It is black colored, five thumbs broad and one cubit and a half high. It is provided with a broad handle and is able to cut buffaloes into pieces. It is lifted with both arms and thrown.[36]

7. The *āstara* (scatterer, bumarang) has a knot at the foot, a long head and is a hand broad. Its middle part is bent to the extent of a cubit, it is sharp, black colored and two cubits long. Whirling, pulling, and breaking are it's three actions, and it is a good weapon for charioteers and foot soldiers.[37]

The general belief is that the bumarang is a weapon peculiar to the Australians; but this is by no means the case. It is well known in many parts of India, especially in its Southern Peninsula. The Tamulian Maravar and Kallar employ it when hunting and throw it after deer. In the

---

12. Nīlalohitavarṇam tat triraśrica susatsaru
ṣoḍaṣāṅgulyunnatam ca tīkṣnāgram pṛthumadhyakam.
13. Satkṛtya manave dattam mahendreṇa samudrikam
prabhutvasūcake loke rājñām gośīrṣamudrike.
14. Muṣṭigrahaḥ parikṣepaḥ paridhiḥ parikuntanam
catvāryetāni gośīrṣe valgitāni pracakṣate.

[35] *See* Ibidem, II. 19; V. 15–17.

15. Asidhenusamākhyātā hastaunnatyapramāṇataḥ
atalatratsaruyutā śyāmā koṭitrayāśritā.
16. Aṅgulidvayavistīrṇā hyāsannaripughātinī
mekhalāgranthinī sā tu projyate khaḍgaputrikā.
17. Muṣṭyagragrahaṇam caiva pāṭanam kuntanam tathā
valgitatrayavatyeṣā sadā dhāryā nṛpottamaiḥ.

[36] *See* Ibidem, II. 19; V. 18, 19.

18. Lavitram bhugnakāyam syāt pṛṣṭhe guru puraśśitam
śyāmam pañcāṅgulivyāmam sārdhahastasamunnatam.
19. Tsaruṇā guruṇā naddham mahiṣādinikartanam
bāhudvayodyamakṣepau lavitre valgite mate.

[37] *See* Ibidem, II. 19; V. 20, 21.

20. Āstaro granthipādassyāt dīrghamaulirbṛhatkaraḥ
bhugnahastodaraśśitaḥ śyāmavarṇo dvihastakaḥ.
21. Bhrāmaṇam karṣaṇam caiva troṭanam tat trivalgitam
jñātvā śatrūn raṇe hanyāt dhāryassādipadātikaiḥ.

Madras Government Museum are shown three bumarangs, two ivory ones, which came from the armoury of the late Rāja of Tanjore, and a common wooden one, which hails from Pudukoṭa. The wood of which the bumarang is made is very dark. I possess four black wooden and one iron bumarang, which I have received from Pudukoṭa. In the arsenal of the Pudukoṭa Rāja is always kept a stock of these sticks. Their name in Tamil is *valai taḍi* (வளை தடி) bent stick, as the stick is bent and flat. When thrown a whirling motion is imparted to the weapon which causes it to return to the place from which it was thrown. The natives are well acquainted with this peculiar fact. The length of the *āstara* or bumarang is not always exactly the same, the difference amounts often to more than one cubit.

8. The *kunta* (lance) has an iron body, a sharp top, and six edges. It is six or ten cubits high, and is round at the foot end. It is handled in six ways.[38]

9. The *sthūṇa* (anvil) has a red body and many knots standing near to each other; it is as high as a man, and straight. It is whirled and fells the enemy to the ground.[39]

10. The *prāsa* (spear) is seven cubits long and made of bamboo, which is colored red. It has a head made of metal, and is sharp at the foot end; it is adorned with silken tufts. Four movements are prescribed for it. In the Śukranīti it resembles a broad sword.[40]

---

[38] *See* Ibidem, II. 19 ; V. 22, 23.

22. Kuntastvayomayāṅgassyāt tīkṣṇaśṛṅgaḥ ṣaḍaśṛmān
pañcahastasamutsedho vṛttapādo bhayaṅkaraḥ.

23. Uddīnam avaḍīnam ca niḍīnam bhūmilīnakam
tiryaglīnam nikhātam ca ṣaḍmārgāḥ kuntam āśritāḥ

Compare Śukranīti, Chapter V, śl. 155.

[39] *See* Ibidem, II. 20 ; V. 24.

24. Sthūṇastu raktadehassyāt samīpadṛḍhaparvakaḥ
pumpramāṇa ṛjustasmin bhramaṇam pātanam dvayam.

[40] *See* Ibidem, II. 20 ; V. 25, 26.

25. Prāsastu saptahastassyāt aunnatyena tu vaiṇavaḥ
lohaśīrṣastīkṣṇapādaḥ kauśeyastabakāñcitaḥ.

11. The *pināka* or *triśūla* (trident) has three heads, is sharp in front, made of brass, has an iron head, and measures four cubits. It has a tuft made of the hair of a bear, and its neck is ornamented with brass armlets. It is shaken and impales the enemy.[41]

12. The *gadā* (club) is made of sharp iron, has 100 spikes at its broad head, and is covered on the sides with spikes. It is a formidable weapon, four cubits long, and its body equals a carriage axle in measure. The head is adorned with a crest; it is covered with a golden belt, and is able to crush elephants and mountains. Twenty different motions are ascribed to the gadā.[42] By means of gunpowder it is thrown out of projectile weapons of various forms.[43]

13. The *mudgara* (hammer) is small at the foot end, has no face, and is three cubits long. Its color resembles

---

26. Ākarṣaśca vikarṣaśca dhūnanam vedhanam tathā
catasra etā gatayo raktaprāsam samāśritāḥ.

Compare Śukranīti, Chapter V, śl. 155.

[41] *See* Ibidem, II. 20; V. 27, 28.

27. Pinākastu triśirṣassyāt śitāgraḥ krūralocanaḥ
kāṁsyakāyo lohaśīrṣaścaturhastapramāṇavān.

28. Ṛkṣaromastabakako jhallivalayagrīvavān
dhūnanam mrotanam ceti triśūlam dve śrite gatī.

Compare Śukranīti, Chapter V, śl. 156, and Agnipurāṇa, 151, 9.

[42] *See* Ibidem, II. 20; V. 29–34.

29. Gadā śaikyāyasamayī śatārapṛthuśīrṣakā
śaṅkuprāvaraṇā ghorā caturhastasamunnatā.

30. Rathākṣamātrakāyā ca kirīṭāñcitamastakā
suvarṇamekhalā guptā gajaparvatabhedinī.

31. Maṇḍalāni vicitrāṇi gatapratyāgatāni ca
astrayantrāṇi citrāṇi sthānāni vividhāni ca.

32. Parimokṣam praharaṇam varjanam paridhāvanam
abhidravaṇam ākṣepam avasthānam savigraham.

33. Parāvṛttam sannivṛttam avaplutam upaplutam
dakṣiṇam maṇḍalam caiva savyam maṇḍalam eva ca.

34. Aviddham ca praviddham ca sphoṭanam jvālanam tathā
upanyastam apanyastam gadā margāśca viṁśatiḥ.

Compare Agnipurāṇa, 151, 12.

[43] The word Astrayantrāṇi (*see* v. 31-b) is explained in the old commentary accompanying the Nītiprakāśikā as "astravatagnyādinirmāṇaprayuktapreraṇāni."

honey, its shoulder is broad, and it weighs eight loads.[44] It has a good handle, is round, black colored, and is a hand in circumference. It is whirled around and fells things to the ground.[45]

14. The *sīra* (ploughshare) is doubly curved, has no head, but an iron-plated front, and crushes the objects with which it comes into contact. It equals a man in height, is of agreeable color, and by means of much dragging it causes persons and things to fall to the ground.[46]

15. The *musala* (pestle) has neither eyes nor head, neither hands nor feet. It is well joined together at both ends and fells and crushes enemies.[47]

16. The *paṭṭiśa* (battle-axe) is of a man's height, has two sharp blades and a sharp top. Its handle has a protection for the hand. The paṭṭiśa is generally called the uterine brother of the sword.[48]

17. The *mauṣṭika* (fist-sword, dagger) has a good hilt, is a span long and ornamented. Its end is sharp, it has a high neck, is broad in the midst and dark colored. It can make

---

[44] A load or *bhāra* is generally estimated to be equal to 20 tulas = 2,000 palas of gold, or between 140—150 pounds.

[45] *See* Ibidem, II. 20; V. 35, 36.

35. Mudgarassūkṣmapādassyāt hīnaśīrṣastrihastavān
madhuvarṇaḥ pṛthuskandhaścāṣṭabhāraguruśca saḥ.

36. Satsarurvartulo nīlo paridhyā karasammitaḥ
bhrāmaṇam pātanam ceti dvividham mudgareśritam.

Compare Agnipurāṇa, 151, 14.

[46] *See* Ibidem, II. 20; V. 37.

37. Sīro dvivakro viśikho lohapaṭṭamukhaḥ kṛṣan
pumpramāṇaḥ snigdhavarṇaḥ svākarṣavinipātavān.

[47] *See* Ibidem, II. 20: V 38.

38. Musalastvakṣiśīrṣābhyām karaiḥ pādairvivarjitaḥ
mūle cāntetisambandhaḥ pātanam prothanam dvayam.

[48] *See* Ibidem, II. 20; V. 39.

39. Paṭṭiśaḥ pumpramāṇassyāt dvidhārastīkṣṇaśṛṅgakaḥ
hastatrāṇasamāyuktamuṣṭiḥ khaḍgasahodaraḥ.

Compare Śukranīti, Chapter V, śl. 153, and Agnipurāṇa, 151, 16.

all sorts of movements, as it is a small and very handy weapon. Its qualities are enlarged upon by Vaiśampāyana.[49]

18. The *parigha* (battering ram) is of a round shape, as big as a palmyra-tree, and of good wood. Experts know, that a whole troop is required to make it move and strike.[50]

19. The *mayūkhī* (pole) is a staff, has a hilt, and is of the height of a man. It is covered with bells, exhibits various colors, and is provided with a shield as a friend. It is used for striking, for warding off a blow, for killing, for discharging and for attacking.[51]

20. The *śataghnī* (hundred-killer) is provided with thorns, is of black iron, and hard. It looks like a mudgara, is four cubits long, round and provided with a handle. According to Vaiśampāyana it resembles in all its movements the gadā, it was therefore like the gadā shot out of other projectile weapons. According to others it is itself a projectile weapon, a great cannon. The name states only its destructiveness, and leaves its nature doubtful; but if it was hurled out of

---

[49] *See* Ibidem, II. 20; V. 40–44.

40. Mauṣṭikaṁ satsarurjñeyam prādeśonnati bhūṣitam
    śitāgram unnatagrīvam pṛthūdaram sitam tathā.
41. Maṇḍalāni vicitrāṇi sthānāni vividhāni ca
    gomūtrakāni citrāṇi gatapratyāgatāni ca.
42. Tiraścīnagatānyeva tathā vakragatāni ca
    parimokṣam praharaṇam varjanam paridhāvanam.
43. Abhidravaṇam āplāvam adhassthānam savigraham
    parāvṛttam apāvṛttam apadrutam apaplutam.
44. Upanyastam apanyastam āghātam sthālanam tathā
    ētāni valgitānyāhurmauṣṭike nṛpasattama.

Compare Śukranīti, Chapter V, śl. 153.

[50] *See* Ibidem, II. 20; V. 45.

45. Parigho vartulākārastālamātrasutāravaḥ
    balaikasādhyasampātaḥ tasmin jñeyo vicakṣanaiḥ.

[51] *See* Ibidem, II. 20; V. 46, 47.

46. Mayūkhī kṛtayaṣṭissyāt muṣṭiyuktā naronnatā
    kiṅkiṇīsaṁvṛtā citrā phalikā sahacāriṇī.
47. Āghātam ca pratīghātam vighātam parimocanam
    abhidravaṇam ityete mayūkhīm pañca saṁśritāḥ.

enormous tubes by means of gunpowder, it must have been a very formidable projectile.[52]

These twenty weapons, belonging to the amukta division, are deposited in the second foot of the Dhanurveda.

All these thirty-two weapons were, according to tradition, taken from the body of the sage Dadhīci. And this is the way how it happened :—

When the gods had been defeated by the demons in a great battle, which defeat they owed in some part to their insufficient knowledge of the Dhanurveda, they perceived on their flight the great sage Dadhīci, who was sitting near the place they passed. To him they entrusted their arms and continued their flight until they reached the high mountain Mandara, under whose bulky body they sought and obtained an asylum. Here they rested for many years, acknowledging Indra as their immediate superior. The sage meanwhile guarded well these weapons, which through his penance had all been changed into spikes, had entered his body and had become his bones. Thus a long time passed away, until the gods became at last anxious to recover once more their lost position and to try another fight with the demons. In their dejection they appeared before Brahma, the father of all beings, and requested him to help them. Brahma, moved to pity, imparted to them the Dhanurveda, together with the spells and all the necessary implements belonging to it. Supplied with the Dhanurveda, his four feet and his six aṅgas, the gods went in search of Dadhīci and requested him to surrender to them their weapons. Dadhīci was quite willing to do so, even though this kindness should cost him his life, provided he were allowed to ascend to the divine heaven.

---

[52] *See* Ibidem, II. 20 ; V. 48, 49.

48. Śataghnī kaṇṭakayutā kālāyasamayī dṛḍhā
mudgarābhā caturhastā vartulā tsaruṇā yutā.

49. Gadā valgitavatyeṣā mayeti kathitā tava.

His request was granted, and Dadhīci advised the gods to let a cow lick his body until the bones which represented their arms were laid free. This was done. Out of the thirty-one bones of Dadhīci's body arose thirty-one weapons, and his backbone, the thirty-second bone, was transformed into the thirty-second weapon, Indra's thunderbolt.[53] Provided with these weapons, which had assumed the shape of the bones from which they originated, the gods went to encounter the demons again, who could not withstand this time the assault of the gods.

But the mouth of the cow, as it had been guilty of the great sin of Brahman-murder, became henceforth an object of abhorrence to the pious; and up to this day orthodox Brahmans when meeting a cow, try to avoid looking at its head, and endeavour to let their eyes fall previously on the hinder part of its body.[54]

One of the most important weapons, the *khaḍga* or *asi*, *i.e.*, the sword, is not included in these two lists, because being created separately and specially by Brahma, it was regarded as a superior weapon altogether.

The high estimation in which the khaḍga was held by Vaiśampāyana is not apparent in the Agnipurāṇa, where it is classed as a rather inferior weapon. Tradition says that it was given to Indra to be used against the Asuras. According to its nature the khaḍga belongs to the second or *amukta* class.[55]

---

[53] *See* Ibidem II. 43–60 ; Mahābhārata, V, 8695 ; IX, 2949, &c.

[54] *See* Ibidem, II. 54, 55.

54. Gomukham brahmahatyāpi viveśa nṛpasattama
devasantoṣaṇāt lokān śāśvatān śa ṛṣiryayau.

55. Tadāprabhṛti lokā vai na paśyantīha gomukham
prātaḥ puruṣaśārdula taddoṣagatamānasāḥ.

[55] *See* Agnipurāṇa, 148, v. 5 and 8.

5. Khaḍgādikam amuktam ca niyuddham vigatāyudham.

8. Tāni khaḍgajaghanyāni bāhupratyavarāṇi ca.

The story goes, that when the gods were battling against the demons, there appeared through Brahma's agency on the top of the Himālaya mountain the deity of the sword, the *Asidevatā*, illuminating by its splendour the whole sky, the earth at the same time was shaking to its very foundation. The *khaḍga* was thus introduced into the world by Brahma for the sake of freeing the universe from the mighty demons. It was 50 thumbs long and 4 broad, and Brahma entrusted it to Śiva or Rudra. After success had attended the undertaking of Śiva, he delivered the sword to Viṣṇu, who on his side handed it over again to Marīci and the other sages. One of the latter, the sage Ṛṣabha, gave it to Indra. Indra conferred it on the guardians of the quarters of the world, and these latter presented it to Manu, the son of the Sun, to help him in the administration of justice against evil-doers. Since that time it has remained in the family of Manu. The constellation of the khaḍga is the Kṛttikā, its deity Agni, the head of its gotra Rohiṇī, and its supreme deity is Rudra. Besides Nistriṁśā it has the eight following different names: *Asi*, *Viśamana*, *Khaḍga*, *Tīkṣṇadharma*, *Durāsada*, *Śrīgarbha*, *Vijaya* and *Dharmamūla*. It is handled in thirty-two different ways, and carried on the left side.

The third species of weapons, the *Muktāmukta*, those which may be thrown and not thrown are divided into two classes, into the Sopasaṁhāra or those which are connected with the withdrawing or restraining Upasaṁhāra and into the Upasaṁhāra themselves, which are the restrainers of the previous class.[56]

Of the former there are 44 varieties, and of the latter 54.

Ibidem, 149, 7, 8; 150, 1–5; Compare Śukranīti, Chapter V, śl. 154, 155; and Nītiprakāśikā III, 1–40. The third book of the Nītiprakāśikā is entirely devoted to the khaḍga. Compare ibidem also, II. 12a.

12a. Muktam bāṇādi vijñeyam khaḍgādikam amuktakam.

[56] The Sopasaṁhāra and Upasaṁhāra weapons are almost identical with the lists of arms presented by Viśvāmitra to Rāma as we read in the Bālakāṇḍa (in Schlegel's edition, cantos 29 and 30; in the old Calcutta edition,

The 44 Sopasaṁhāra weapons are the following :—

1. The *daṇḍacakra* (discus of punishment).
2. The *dharmacakra* (the discus of right).
3. The *kālacakra* (the discus of Yama).
4. The *aindracakra* (the discus of Indra).
5. The *śūlavara* (the spear of Śiva).
6. The *brahmaśīrṣa* (the head of Brahma).

---

canto 26). The latter edition contains more names than Schlegel's. The enumeration contained in Vaiśampāyana's Nītiprakāśikā is independent of that of the Rāmāyaṇa, and for that very reason it is peculiarly interesting. It is therefore here given in the original; Nītiprakāśikā, II. 22–37.

22. Daṇḍacakram dharmacakram kālacakram tathaiva ca
aindracakram śūlavaram brahmaśīrṣam ca modakī.
23. Śikharī dharmapāśam ca tathā varuṇapāśakam
painākāstram ca vāyavyam śuṣkārdre, śikharāstrakam.
24. Krauñcāstram hayaśīrṣam ca divyādivye'strasañjñike
gāndharvāstram nandanāstram varṣaṇam śoṣaṇam tathā.
25. Prasvāpanapraśamane santāpanavilāpane
mathanaṁ mānavāstram ca sāmanam tāmasam tathā.
26. Saṁvartam mausalam satyam sauram māyāstram eva ca
tvāṣṭram astram ca somāstram saṁhāram mānasam tathā.
27. Nāgāstram gāruḍāstram ca śaileṣīkeśtrasañjñike
catuścatvāri caitāni sopasaṁhārakāṇi vai.
28. Vakṣyāmi copasaṁhārān kramaprāptān nibodhame
yān jñātvā vairimuktāni cāstrāṇi śamayiṣyasi (*Pṛthu*).
29. Satyavān satyakīrtiśca rabhaso dhṛṣṭa eva ca
pratihāratarаścaivāpyavāṅmukhaparāṅmukhau.
30. Dṛḍhanābho' lakṣyalakṣyāvāvilaśca sunābhakaḥ
daśākṣaśśatavaktraśca daśaśīrṣaśatodarau.
31. Dharmanābho mahānābho dundunābhastu nābhakaḥ
jyotiṣavimalau caiva nairāśyakarśanāvubhau.
32. Yogandharaḥ sanidraśca daityaḥ pramathanastathā
sārcirmālī dhṛtirmālī vṛttimān rucirastathā.
33. Pitryassaumanasaścaiva vidhūtamakarau tathā
karavīro dhanaratī dhānyam vai kāmarūpakaḥ.
34. Jṛmbakāvaraṇam caiva mohaḥ kāmarucistathā.
varuṇaḥ sarvadamanaḥ sandhānaḥ sarpanāthakaḥ.
35. Kaṅkālāstram mausalāstram kāpālāstram ca kaṅkaṇam
paiśācāstram ceti pañcāpyasurāstrāṇi bhūpate.
36. Satyavān sarvadamanaḥ kāmarūpastathaiva ca
yogandharopyalakṣyaścāpyasurāstravighātakāḥ.
37. Catuścatvāriṁśat ete pañcānyonyavimardanāḥ
melayitvā ca pañcāśat ekonāhyastraśamakāḥ.
38. Sarvamocananāmā tu suprabhātanayo mahān
muktāmuktākhilaśamo madvarāt prathitaḥ paraḥ.

7. The *modakī* (the charmer).
8. The *śikharī* (the pointed).
9. The *dharmapāśa* (the noose of right).
10. The *varuṇapāśa* (the noose of Varuṇa).
11. The *paīnākāstra* (the missile of Śiva).
12. The *vāyavya* (the missile of Vāyu).
13. The *śuṣka* (the dry).
14. The *ārdra* (the wet).
15. The *śikharāstra* (the flaming missile).
16. The *krauñcāstra* (the Krauñca missile).
17. The *hayaśīrṣa* (the horse-headed missile).
18. The *vidyāstra* (the missile of knowledge).
19. The *avidyāstra* (the missile of ignorance).
20. The *gandharvāstra* (the gandharva missile).
21. The *nandanāstra* (the joy-producing missile).
22. The *varṣaṇa* (the rainy missile).
23. The *śoṣaṇa* (the drying missile).
24. The *prasvāpana* (the sleep-causing missile).
25. The *praśamana* (the soothing missile).
26. The *santāpana* (the tormenting missile).
27. The *vilāpana* (the wailing missile).
28. The *mathana* (the churning missile).
29. The *mānavāstra* (the missile of Manu).
30. The *sāmana* (the conciliatory missile).
31. The *tāmasa* (the missile of darkness).
32. The *saṁvarta* (the rolling missile).
33. The *mausala* (the club-shaped missile).
34. The *satya* (the missile of truth).
35. The *saura* (the missile of the sun).
36. The *māyāstra* (the missile of illusion).
37. The *tvāṣṭra* (the missile of Viśvakarma)
38. The *somāstra* (the missile of the moon).
39. The *saṁhāra* (the missile of restraining).
40. The *mānasa* (the spiritual missile).
41. The *nāgāstra* (the missile of the serpent).
42. The *garuḍāstra* (the missile of Garuḍa).

43. The *śailāstra* (the rocky missile).
44. The *iṣīkāstra* (the reed missile).

The 55 Upasaṁhāra weapons are as follows :—

1. The *satyavān* (the true).
2. The *satyakīrti* (the truly-famed)
3. The *rabhasa* (the impetuous).
4. The *dhṛṣṭa* (the bold).
5. The *pratihāra* (the warding off).
6. The *avāṅmukha* (the downfaced).
7. The *parāṅmukha* (the averted face).
8. The *dṛḍhanābha* (the weapon with firm navel).
9. The *alakṣya* (the imperceptible).
10. The *lakṣya* (the perceptible).
11. The *āvila* (the turbid).
12. The *sunābhaka* (the weapon with good navel).
13. The *daśākṣa* (the ten-eyed).
14. The *śatavaktra* (the hundred-mouthed).
15. The *daśaśīrṣa* (the ten-headed).
16. The *śatodara* (the hundred-bellied).
17. The *dharmanābha* (the weapon with the navel of right).
18. The *mahānābha* (the big-navelled).
19. The *dundunābha* (the drum-navelled).
20. The *nābhaka* (the navelled).
21. The *jyotiṣa* (the luminous).
22. The *vimala* (the stainless).
23. The *nairāśya* (the discourager).
24. The *karśaṇa* (the emaciating).
25. The *yogandhara* (the united).
26. The *sanidra* (the sleeping).
27. The *daitya* (the fiendish).
28. The *pramathana* (the churner).
29. The *sārcirmālā* (the garland of energy).
30. The *dhṛti* (the supporting).
31. The *mālī* (the necklaced).
32. The *vṛttima* (the abiding).

33. The *rucira* (the glittering).
34. The *pitrya* (the paternal).
35. The *saumanasa* (the good-minded).
36. The *vidhūta* (the vibrating).
37. The *makara* (the monster).
38. The *karavīra* (the scymitar).
39. The *dhanarati* (the desire of wealth).
40. The *dhānya* (the grain).
41. The *kāmarūpaka* (the shape-assumer).
42. The *jṛmbaka* (the gaper).
43. The *āvaraṇa* (the protecting).
44. The *moha* (the fascinating).
45. The *kāmaruci* (following one's own wishes).
46. The *vāruṇa* (the missile of Varuṇa).
47. The *sarvadamana* (the all-subduer).
48. The *sandhāna* (the aimer).
49. The *sarpanāthaka* (the missile belonging to the god of serpents).
50. The *kaṅkālāstra* (the skeleton missile).
51. The *mausalāstra* (the pestle missile).
52. The *kāpālāstra* (the skull missile).
53. The *kaṅkaṇa* (the bracelet weapon).
54. The *paiśācāstra* (the infernal missile).

The Sopasaṁhāra weapons are contained in the 29th Sarga of Schlegel's edition of the Bālakāṇḍa, while the Upasaṁhāra weapons are mentioned mostly in the 30th canto.

The last five weapons are peculiar to the demons, while five other weapons are on the other hand most effective against these demons and cause their destruction; they are found under the numbers 1, 9, 25, 41, and 47.

These 44 Sopasaṁhāra and 54 Upasaṁhāra weapons represent the Muktāmukta class, and they are deposited in the third foot of the Dhanurveda. They represent the belief so widely spread in India that the knowledge of certain spells endowed their owner with supernatural power, of which power these mysterious weapons are the outward token. To a per son not within the pale of Brahmanism they appear like mere creations of a fervid imagination. On the other hand the Indians do not stand alone in this belief in supernatural weapons, though it has been reserved to them only to define and to classify them methodically.

The last and most potent division, or the Mantramukta, is only represented by six weapons, but then they are so powerful that nothing can frustrate or subdue them. Their names are—

1. *Viṣṇucakra* (the discus of Viṣṇu).
2. *Vajrāstra* (the thunderbolt).
3. *Brahmāstra* (the missile of Brahma).
4. *Kālapāśaka* (the noose of death).
5. *Nārāyaṇāstra* (the missile of Nārāyaṇa).
6. *Pāśupatāstra* (the missile of Paśupati).

These six weapons, which are projected by spells, reside in his fourth foot.[57]

When Vaiśampāyana has finished in his second chapter the enumeration of the weapons, which he assigns to the four different classes, and has given in the following three chapters an accurate description of the sword and all the thirty-two arms belonging to the two first divisions, he remarks that the efficiency of the weapons varies and is subject to great changes. In different ages and at different places the quality of a weapon is not the same, for the mode of construction and the material out of which it is made is of a different kind. Moreover much depends on the strength and the ability of the person who uses such arms in increasing, preserving or diminishing their efficiency.[58]

In addition to these weapons others were in actual use, but they are said to be specially peculiar to the lowest or

---

[57] *See* Nītiprakāśikā, II. 40.

40. Viṣṇucakram vajram astram brahmāstram kālapāśakam
nārāyaṇam pāśupatam nāśāmyam itarāstrakaiḥ.

[58] *See* Nītiprakāśikā, V. 51.

51. Etāni vikṛtim yānti yugaparyāyato nṛpa
dehadārḍhyānusāreṇa tathā buddhyanusārataḥ.

fourth age, the Kaliyuga, in which we live. Though these four ages or *yugas* are nowhere mentioned in the ancient Vedic literature, and though the constitution of the great or *Mahāyuga* is most probably an invention of a comparatively later period—perhaps after the commencement of the Kaliyuga had been connected with a certain date and the other yugas had been reckoned backwards from that date—it is a most singular phenomenon that many otherwise enlightened Brahmans really believe that they possess records from these previous three yugas.

The assumption of the depravity of the existing Kaliyuga and the superiority of the preceding ages is consoling to the feeling of those who no longer occupy the same exalted position as formerly, and who try to insinuate that the cause of the loss of their prestige is neither due to their own faults nor to the superiority of their rulers, but to the decrees of fate, to which every one is subject. We can here dispense with the presumption that the arms of any particular yuga are good or bad in the same proportion as the yuga itself is good or bad, the more so as a good and really auspicious age, from its intrinsic goodness, does not require any weapons to protect it ; as in such a happy era righteousness and prosperity prevail everywhere.

But even in the Kaliyuga humanity is not so debased that no voice is raised against the use of cruel and barbarous weapons. On the other hand wherever and whenever arms are used, the object of their use must have been to apply force, either for offensive or defensive purposes. Remembering this fact one need not wonder that but little humanity is as a rule displayed in restraining the efficiency of weapons, and though, as we shall see, the ancient Hindu law books objected strongly to the use of certain arms, it is doubtful whether this prohibition was in reality ever enforced, for there exists a difference between uttering sentiments creditable to humanity and enforcing them in practice.

On the other hand we meet occasionally precepts which certainly do not exhibit a great amount of human kindness. Thus we read in the Pañcatantra: "By a wise man should an enemy be killed, even if he be his son-in-law; if no other means be possible, he who murders commits no sin. A soldier who goes to the battle does not think about right and wrong; Dhṛṣṭadyumna was in olden times murdered in his sleep by the son of Droṇa."[59]

The war machines which the ancient Indians used, whether they were made of metal or of stone, and out of which they hurled iron and lead balls at their enemies, were doubtless discharged by means of gunpowder. The existence of gunpowder is intimated by Vaiśampāyana in his description of the nalikā and by the application of smoke-balls which, according to the commentator of Vaiśampāyana, were really made of gunpowder.[60] The ancient Hindus were also, as is well known, great adepts in the art of smelting and casting metals.

The old Hindus displayed a great ingenuity in inventing injurious and irritating compounds and refined expedients for hurling them amongst the enemy during a combat.[61]

Boiling oil has been used by many nations in different parts of the globe, and the old Indians believed also in its efficacy, but they used besides explosive oil. The resin of the Śāl tree (*Shorea robusta*), which resin is also called *kalakala*, is recommended likewise. The casting of melted sugar is mentioned as well as that of heated sand. Pots filled with venomous snakes mixed together with honey, spikes and big stones, saws, smoke-balls, burning husks of corn, and other injurious preparations were frequently employed in India.

---

[59] *See* Pañcatantra, I. 299, 300.

[60] Dhūmagulika is explained by Cūrṇagola, powderball.

[61] *See* Nītiprakāśikā, V. 52.

52. Yantrāṇi lohasīsānām gulikākṣepakāṇi ca
tathā copalayantrāṇi kṛtrimāṇyaparāṇi ca.

The soldiers of Duryodhana, when encamped in Kurukṣetra, had at their disposal similar implements of war.[62]

These weapons and mixtures were probably used more generally during sieges and in street-fights than in open combat.

The weapons just now enumerated and many others of the same objectionable and cruel type are ascribed to the depravity of the Kaliyuga, when war is conducted in an unfair, mean, and deceitful manner. The existence of many uncivilized nations of the lowest origin contributes greatly to the degeneration of the times. Among the despicable peoples thus enumerated are found the Huns, Pulindas, Śabaras, Pahlavas, Śakas, Mālavas, Varvaras, Koṅkaṇas, Āndhras, Colas, Pāṇḍyas, Keralas, Mlecchas, Caṇḍālas, Śvapacas, Khalas, Mavellakas, Lalitthas,[63] Kirātas, and Kukkuras. To add insult to injury, and to show the low position of these nations, the Hindus said these tribes originated from the vagina of a cow.[64]

---

[62] *See* Ibidem, V. 53, 54.

53. Kūṭayuddhasahāyāni bhaviṣyanti kalau nṛpa
taptatailam sarjarasam guḍalālo gravālukā.

54. Madhusāśīviṣaghaṭāḥ śilakāni bṛhacchilāḥ
krakacā dhūmagulikāḥ tuṣāṅgārādikam tathā.

Compare, Mahābhārata, Udyogaparva, Adhyāya, 155, 5-7.

5. Sakacagrahavikṣepāḥ satailaguḍavālukāḥ
saśīviṣaghaṭāḥ sarve sasarjarasapāṁsavaḥ.

6. Saṅghaṭaphalakāḥ sarve sāyoguḍajalopalāḥ
saśālabhindipālāśca samadūcchiṣṭamudgarāḥ.

7. Sakāṇḍadaṇḍakāḥ sarve sasīraviṣatomarāḥ.
saśūrpapiṭakāḥ sarve sadātrāṅkuśatomarāḥ.

[63] *See* Ibidem, V, 55-57.

55. Hūnāḥ pulindāḥ śabarā varvarā pahlavāḥ śakāḥ
mālavāḥ koṅkaṇā ḥyāndhrāḥ colāḥ pāṇḍyāḥ sakeralāḥ.

56. Mlecchā goyonayaścānye caṇḍālāḥ śvapacāḥ khalāḥ
māvellakā lalitthāśca kirātāḥ kukkurāḥ tathā.

57. Pāpā hyete katham dharmam vetsyanti ca viyonayaḥ
saṅkaryadoṣaniratā bhaviṣyantyadhame yuge.

[64] Most of these names appear also in the Mahābhārata and Rāmāyaṇa. The Hindus call the modern Europeans, *Huns*, this expression most probably arose from the idea that the ancient Hunnish invaders came also from Europe. The 14th Chapter of the Harivaṁśa contains an enumeration of many barbarous nations.

CHAPTER II.

ON THE AUTHENTICITY OF THE ŚUKRANĪTI.

The reputed author of the Śukranīti—a chapter from which on the army organisation and the political maxims of the ancient Hindus we shall give further on in these pages—is Uśanas or Śukra. He is also called Maghābhava, Kavi, Kāvya, Bhārgava, Ṣoḍaśārcis, Daityaguru, and Dhiṣṇya.[65] According to some he is the son or descendant of Bhṛgu, and, therefore, he is named Bhārgava; to others he is known as Kavi or the poet, and to others also as Kāvya, the son of Kavi, a son of Bhṛgu. He is regarded as the regent of the planet Venus or Śukra; and the Śukravāra or Friday is named after him; his connection with this planet is also evident in his names Maghābhava, Ṣoḍaśārcis, and Dhiṣṇya. Moreover he is the preceptor of the Daityas or Demons and is called therefore Daityaguru. Bṛhaspati, the preceptor of the gods and the regent of the planet Jupiter, is like Śukra the author of a famous Daṇḍanīti, or a work on civil and military administration. This work of Śukra is highly praised in the Kāmandakīya, as containing the principles of all sciences, and its ślokas are very often found in the Kāmandakīya.[66]

Throughout Indian literature Śukra is always upheld as one of the greatest sages, his sayings are carefully noted and quotations from his Essence of Polity or Nītisāra are met with in the most ancient and celebrated writings.

---

[65] *See* "Śukro Maghābhavaḥ Kāvya Uśanā Bhārgavaḥ Kaviḥ Ṣoḍaśārcir Daityagurur Dhiṣṇyaḥ," in Hemacandra's *Anekārtharatnamālā*, II, 33 and 34; compare Amarakoṣa, I, 1, 26; and Halāyudha's Abhidhānaratnamālā, I, 48; &c. &c.

[66] *See* Kāmandakīya, II, 4, 5.

4. Vārtā ca daṇḍanītiśca dve vidye ityavasthite
   lokasyārthapradhānatvāt śiṣyāḥ surapurodhasaḥ.

5. Ekaiva daṇḍanītistu vidye tyauśanasī sthitiḥ
   tasyām tu sarvavidyānām ārambhāḥ samudāhṛtāḥ.

The reason of calling Śukra's work a *Daṇḍanīti* is explained in Śukranīti, I, 157, as follows:—

Damo daṇḍa iti khyātastasmāt daṇḍo mahīpatiḥ
tasya nītirdaṇḍanītirnayanāt nītirucyate.

The author of the Śukranīti is very frequently mentioned in the Mahābhārata. In one place we read that Brahma wrote the first Daṇḍanīti which contained the enormous number of 100,000 chapters. This bulky volume was reduced by Śaṅkara or Śiva into a code called Viśālākṣa which still comprehended 10,000 chapters. Indra reduced the Viśālākṣa into the Bāhudaṇḍaka which reached the respectable number of 5,000 chapters. Indra was followed by Bṛhaspati, whose Bārhaspatya amounted to 3,000 chapters. Kāvya or Uśanas thinking that the life of man was too short to digest such enormous books limited his Nītisāra to 1,000 chapters.[67] It was thus Uśanas, who made the Daṇḍanīti accessible to men.

---

[67] *See* Mahābhārata, Śāntiparva, Rājadharma, LIX, 28, 29, 76–87.

28. Tān uvāca surān sarvān Svayambhūr bhagavānstataḥ
 śreyo'ham cintayiṣyāmi vyetuvobhīḥ surarṣabhāḥ.

29. Tatodhyāyasahasrāṇām śatam cakre svabuddhijam
 yatra dharmastathaivārthaḥ kāmaścaivābhivarṇitaḥ.

76. Etat kṛtvā śubham śāstram tataḥ subhagavān prabhuḥ
 devān uvāca saṁhṛṣṭaḥ tataḥ Śakrapurogamān.

77. Upakārāya lokasya trivargasthāpanāya ca
 navanītam sarasvatyā buddhireṣa prabhāvitā.

78. Daṇḍena sahitāhyeṣā lokarakṣaṇakārikā
 nigrahānugraharatā lokān anucariṣyati.

79. Daṇḍena nīyate cedam daṇḍam nayati vā punaḥ
 daṇḍanītiriti khyātā trilokān abhivartate.

80. Ṣāḍguṇyaguṇasāraiṣā sthāsyatyagre mahātmasu
 dharmārthakāmamokṣāśca sakalā hyatra śabditāḥ.

81. Tatastān bhagavān nītim pūrvam jagrāha Śaṅkaraḥ
 bahurūpo viśālākṣaḥ śivassthāṇurumāpatiḥ.

82. Prajānām āyuṣohrāsam vijñāya bhagavān Śivaḥ
 sañcikṣepa tataḥ śāstram mahārtham brahmaṇā kṛtam.

83. Viśālākṣam iti proktam tad idam pratyapadyata
 daśādhyāyasahasrāṇi Subrahmaṇyo mahātapāḥ.

84. Bhagavān api tacchāstram sañcikṣepa Purandaraḥ.
 sahasraiḥ pañcābhis tāta yaduktam bāhudaṇḍakam.

85. Adhyāyānām sahasraistu tribhireva Bṛhaspatiḥ
 sañcikṣepeśvaro buddhyā Bārhaspatyam yaducyate.

86. Adhyāyānām sahasreṇa Kāvyaḥ saṅkṣepam abravīt
 tacchāstram amṛtoprajño yogācāryo mahāyaśāḥ.

87. Evam lokānurodhena śāstram etanmaharṣibhiḥ
 saṅksiptam āyurvijñāya martyānām hrāsam eva ca

According to the *Nītiprakāśikā* Brahma, Rudra, Subrahmaṇya, Indra, Manu, Bṛhaspati, Śukra, Bhāradvāja, Gauraśiras and Vyāsa were authors of works on polity. Brahma's Daṇḍanīti contained 100,000 chapters, that of Rudra 50,000, that of Subrahmaṇya 25,000, that of Indra 12,000, that of Manu 6,000, that of Bṛhaspati 3,000, that of Śukra 1,000, that of Bhāradvāja 700, that of Gauraśiras 500, and that of Vedavyāsa 300 chapters.[68]

In the second Śloka of the Śukranīti we read that Brahma's work consisted of ten millions of double verses, which would give to each chapter an average length of 100 Ślokas.[69]

Just as the Mānavadharmaśāstra does not contain as many verses, as are said to have been originally in it, so also is the Śukranīti we actually possess by no means as long as is indicated in the Mahābhārata. In fact at the end of the 4th section the Śukranīti is declared to be only 2,200 Ślokas

---

[68] *See* Nītiprakāśikā, I, 21–28.

21. Brahmā maheśvaraḥ skandaścendraprācetaso manuḥ
bṛhaspatiśca śukraśca bhāradvājo mahātapāḥ ;
22. Vedavyāsaśca bhagavān tathā gauraśirā muniḥ
ete hi rājaśāstrāṇām praṇetāraḥ parantapāḥ.
23. Lakṣādhyāyān jagau brahmā rājaśāstre mahāmatiḥ
pañcāśat ca sahasrāṇi rudraḥ saṅkṣipya cābravīt.
24. Pañcaviṁśat sahasrāṇi skandas saṅkṣipya cāvadat
daśādhyāyasahasrāṇi dvisahasre ca vāsavaḥ.
25. Prācetasamanuścāpi ṣaṭsahasrāṇyathābravīt
trīṇyadhyāyasahasrāṇi bṛhaspatiruvāca ha.
26. Kāvyastu tat samālodya cakre'dhyāyasahasrakam
saptādhyāyaśatam śāstram Bhāradvājastathābhaṇat.
27. Munirgauraśirāścāpi pañcādhyāyaśatam jagau
vedavyāsastu bhagavān tat saṅkṣipya mahāmatiḥ
28. Śatatrayādhyāyavatīm nītim cakre mahāmate
saṇkṣiptam āyurvijñāya martyānām buddhidoṣataḥ.

[69] *See* Śukranīti, I, 2–4.

2. Pūrvadevairyathānyāyam nītisāram uvāca tān
śatalakṣaślokamitam nītiśāstram athoktavān.
3. Svayambhūr bhagavān lokahitārtham saṅgraheṇa vai
tatsāram tu Vasiṣṭhādyairasmabhirvṛddhihetave.
4. Alpāyubhūbhṛtādyartham saṅkṣiptam tarkavistṛtam.

long, and it speaks well for the preservation of this ancient work, that though the MSS. differ as to their length in some way or other, the variations in them are not very great. One MS. contains indeed exactly 2,200 ślokas, and all MSS. I possess contain the above verse in question, which thus defines the proportions of the Śukranīti.[70]

In the beginning of the 58th Chapter of the Rājadharma the name of Kāvya occurs also as one of the authors of a Dharmaśāstra, and he is likewise mentioned as such in the second Śloka of the Pañcatantra.[71] The Kāmandakīya and other similar works allude repeatedly to our author. It is a peculiar coincidence that the reason for composing the Śukranīti is the same both in the Śukranīti and in the Mahābhārata. If the former were a later production the cause of this agreement would be evident, but there are many good grounds for the supposition that this is not the case, and that the quotations from Śukra's work on Polity found in such ancient works as the Mahābhārata, Harivaṁśa, Kāmandakīya, Pañcatantra are genuine quotations. A few examples taken at random will be sufficient for our purpose.

The Mahābhārata quotes in the 56th Chapter of the Rājadharmānuśāsana the following as the saying of Uśanas : " A law abiding king should in the exercise of his duties chastise a Brahman, who has even read the whole Veda, who

---

70 *See* Śukranīti, IV, VII. 346.
Manvādyairādṛto yorthastadartho Bhārgaveṇa vai
dvāviṁśatiśatam ślokā nītisāre prakīrtitāḥ.

71 *See* Rājadharma, LVIII, 1–4.
1. Ete te rāja dharmāṇām navanītam Yudhiṣṭhira
Bṛhaspatirhi bhagavān nānyam dharmam praśaṁsati.
2. Viśālākṣaśca bhagavān Kāvyaścaiva mahātapāḥ
sahasrākṣo Mahendraśca tathā Prācetaso Manuḥ.
3. Bhāradvājaśca bhagavān tathā Gauraśirā muniḥ
rājaśāstrapraṇetāro brahmaṇyā brahmavādinaḥ.
4. Rakṣām eva praśaṁsanti dharmam dharmavṛtam vara.
See also Pañcatantram, I, 2.
Manave Vācaspataye Śukrāya Parāśarāya sasutāya
Cāṇakyāya ca viduṣe namo'stu nayaśastrakartṛbhyaḥ.

approaches with uplifted weapons and intent to murder. The king knowing the law should certainly protect the law which is being broken. By such an act he is no law-breaker; for fury recoils on fury." Our Śukranīti expresses this decision (IV, VII, 259) as follows: "He who has raised a weapon against an approaching assassin, even if this be a Vaidika Brahman (Bhrūṇa), and has killed him, should not be considered as a murderer of a Vaidika Brahman; if he has not killed him, he should be regarded as such." [72]

As the śloka of the Śukranīti contains a more difficult reading and the rare term Bhrūna in the sense of Vaidikibrahman occurs here, which is, as it were, explained in the Mahābhārata by "Vēdāntapāraga," there seems to be no doubt which of the two versions is the earlier.[73]

The 57th chapter of the Rājadharma begins with another quotation of Uśanas. He is said to have declared that "the earth swallows these two, namely, a king who does not oppose an enemy and a Brahman who does not travel about, like a snake swallows the animals living in holes."

---

[72] *See* Mahābhārata, Rājadharma, LVI, 27-29.

27. Ślokau cauśanasā gītau purātāta maharṣiṇā
tāu nibodha mahārāja tvam ekāgramanā nṛpa.

28. Udyamya śastram āyāntam api vedāntapāragam
nigṛhṇīyāt svadharmeṇa dharmāpekṣī narādhipaḥ.

29. Vinaśyamānam dharmam hi yo'bhirakṣet sa dharmavit
na tena dharmahā sa syāt manyustanmanyum ṛcchati.

Compare this with Śukranīti, IV, VII, v. 259.

Udyamya śastram āyāntam bhrūṇam apyātatāyinam
nihatya bhrūṇahā na syāt ahatvā bhrūṇahā bhavet.

Compare further with these ślokas, *Manu*, VIII, 350, 351.

[73] That *Bhrūṇahā* means a Vaidika-Brahman murderer is clear from Kullūkabhaṭṭa's Commentary to Manu, VIII, 317 (annāde bhrūṇahā mārṣṭi patyau bhāryāpacāriṇī), for he says there: "Brahmahā yaḥ tatsambandhiyo'nnam atti tasmin asau svapāpam saṅkrāmayati. Bhrūṇahānnabhoktuḥ pāpam bhavatīti. Etad atra vivakṣitam na tu brahmaghnaḥ pāpam naśyati tathā bhāryā vyabhicāriṇī jārapatim kṣamamāṇe bhartari pāpam saṁśleṣayati."

Compare also *Nānārtharatnamālā* by Irugapadaṇḍadhinātha, II, 125, under the word bhrūṇa "Bhrūṇorbhake straiṇagarbhe garbhiṇyām śrotriye dvije."

The Śukranīti contains (IV,VII, 242) this very śloka.[74]

The Harivaṁśa ascribes to Uśanas the wise prescription, that one should never confide in a person whose trustworthiness one has not proved previously, and even to be cautious in giving confidence to a trustworthy person, as the evils of misplaced confidence are serious. This very sentiment, though not quite in the same words, may be found in Śukranīti III, 47–49.[75]

It is peculiar that the Pañcatantra refers these verses on the acquisition of friends to a passage in the Śukranīti, and here,

---

[74] *See* Rājadharma LVII, 1, 2.

1. Bhagavān Uśanā hyāha ślokam atra viśāmpate
tad ihaikamanā rājan gadatastannibodhame.

2. Dvāvimau grasate bhūmiḥ sarpo vilaśayān iva
rājānam cāviyoddhāram brāhmaṇam cāpravāsinam;

in its stead we read in the Śukranīti, IV, VII, 242:

Rājānam cāpayoddhāram brāhmaṇam cāpravāsinam
nirgilati bhūmiretau sarpo vilaśayān iva.

[75] *See* Harivaṁśa XVIII, 127–131.

127. Kusauhṛdena viśvāsaḥ kudeśena prajīvyate
kurājani bhayam nityam kuputre sarvato bhayam.

128. Apakāriṇi visrambham yaḥ karoti narādhamaḥ
anātho durbalo yadvannaciram sa tu jīvati.

129. Na viśvaset aviśvaste viśvaste nātiviśvaset
viśvastāt bhayam utpannam mūlānyapi nikrintati.

130. Rājaseveṣu viśvāsam garbhasaṅkramiteṣu ca
yaḥ karoti naro mūḍho na ciram sa tu jīvati.

131. Abhyunnatim prāpya nṛpaḥ prāvāram kīṭako yathā
sa vinaśyatyasandeham āhaīvam Uśanā nṛpa.

See also Pañcatantram II, 45, and Kāmandakīya, V, 88, 89.

The Śukranīti expresses in the following ślokas, III, 75–80, the same idea:—

75. Bhṛtyo bhrātāpi vā putraḥ patnī kuryāt na caiva yat
vidhāsyanti ca mitrāṇi tat kāryam aviśaṅkitam.

76. Ato yateta tat prāptyai mitralabdhirvarā nṛṇām
nātyantam viśvaset kañcit viśvastam api sarvadā.

77. Putram vā bhrātaram bhāryām amātyam adhikāriṇam
dhanastrī rājyalobho hi sarveṣām adhiko yataḥ.

78. Prāmāṇikam cānubhūtam āptam sarvatra viśvaset
viśvasitvātmavadgūḍhastat kāryam vimṛśet svayam.

79. Tadvākyam tarkato'nartham viparītam na cintayet
catuṣṣaṣṭitamāṁśam tannāśitam kṣamayet athā.

80. Svadharmanītibalavān tena maitrīm pradhārayet
dānairmānaiśca satkāraiḥ supūjyān pūjayet sadā.

III, 76, we find them occurring in connection with this particular subject, the acquisition of friends.[76]

The following Śloka in the Harivaṁśa, which is found a little modified in the Pañcatantra, III, 256, is also ascribed to Uśanas:—"The residue of an enemy, of debt, of fire, O prince! (although scattered) when united, may grow again; therefore one should not allow a residue to remain." The Śukranīti contains nearly the same idea in the same words.[77]

The Kāmandakīya (XII, 67) says that Manu mentions in his law book, that the number of ministers at the court of a king amounts to 12, that Bṛhaspati says it amounts to 16, and that Uśanas fixed it at 20.[78]

In the Śukranīti II, 69 and 70 are as a matter of fact 20 ministers mentioned; *e.g.*, the family priest, vicegerent, chief secretary, war minister, diplomatist, chief justice, learned adviser, finance minister, councillor and ambassador; each of these 10 has a substitute, so that the entire number of ministers amounts to 20.[79]

---

[76] *See* Pañcatantram, II, 47.
Sukṛtyam viṣṇuguptasya mitrāptibhārgavasya ca
bṛhaspater aviśvāso nītisandhistridhā sthitaḥ.

[77] *See* Harivaṁśa, XVIII, 136, 137.
136. Na ca śeṣam prakurvanti punarvairabhayāt narāḥ
ghātayanti samūlam hi śrutvemām upamām nṛpa.
137. Śatruśeṣam ṛṇaśeṣam śeṣam agneśca bhūnṛpa
punarvardheta sambhūya tasmāt śeṣam na śeṣayet.
Compare Śukranīti, III, 101–103.
101. Sarpo'gnirdurjano rājā jāmātā bhāginīsutaḥ
rogaḥ śatrurnāvamānyopyalpa ityupacārataḥ.
102. Krauryāt taikṣṇyadussvabhāvāt svāmitvāt putrikābhayāt
svapūrvajapiṇḍadatvāt vṛddhibhītyā upacaret.
103. Ṛṇaśeṣam rogaśeṣam śatruśeṣam na rakṣayet
yācakādyaiḥ prārthitassan na tīkṣṇam cottaram vadet.

[78] Dvādaśeti Mānuḥ prāha ṣoḍaśeti Bṛhaspatiḥ
Uśanā viṁśatiriti mantriṇām mantramaṇḍalam.

[79] The ślokas in question are as follows:—
69. Purodhāca pratinidhiḥ pradhānassacivastathā
mantrīca prāṅvivākaśca paṇḍitaśca sumantrakaḥ;
70. Amātyo dūta ityetā rājñaḥ prakṛtayo daśa
daśamāṁśadhikāḥ pūrvam dūtāntāḥ kramaśaḥ smṛtāḥ.

The Kāmandakīya (VIII, 22-23) ascribes to Uśanas the observation that the sphere round a king consists of twelve other kings of whom 4 are enemies, 4 friends and 4 neutrals.

A king X, *e.g.*, is surrounded by three circles A, B, C, and in these circles resides one king in each of the four directions of the compass. Immediate neighbours are always hostile to each other, thus a king of the A line is an enemy to his neighbour in the B line, and the same feeling animates B towards his neighbour in C. As X is an enemy to the kings of the A line and the latter are enemies to the kings living in the B circle, X and the B kings become friends by being bound together by their hostility to the A kings, and X and the C kings are neutrals as, they have no interest in common, being too distant from each other. This very idea is well expressed in the Śukranīti, IV, I, 17-18.[80]

The whole Śukranīti is divided into four sections with a fifth supplementary section at the end.

The first section treats on the duties of a king; the second on the position of the crown prince; the third mainly on income and expenditure on servants and wages; the fourth is divided into seven chapters, treating respectively 1, on friendship and (enmity), 2, on the treasury, 3, on administration, 4, on revenue, arts and science, 5, on social laws, 6, on fortresses, and 7, on the army.

This last chapter is given afterwards entirely. It begins with a definition of the word army, goes on to state the different character of the troops; the mode of their movements, whether they march on foot, ride on horses and

[80] *See* Kāmandakīya, VIII, 22, 23.

22. Udāsīno madhyamaśca vijigīṣostu maṇḍalam
uśanā maṇḍalam idam prāha dvādaśarājakam.

23. Dvādaśānām narendrāṇām arimitre pṛthak pṛthak;

and Śukranīti, IV, I, 17, 18.

17. Āsamantāt caturdikṣu sannikṛṣṭāśca ye nṛpāh
tatparāstatparā ye'nye kramāt hīnabalārayah.

18. Śatrūdāsīnamitrāṇi kramāt te syustu prākrtāh
arirmitram udāsīno'nantarastatparasparam.

elephants, or are driven in carriages. Then follows a description of the various kinds of soldiers, and afterwards a description of the animals and conveyances used for army purposes. This is succeeded by a classification of the arms used in warfare and such arms are described. Among these are mentioned firearms and a full account is given of the manufacture of gunpowder. [81] These two subjects will be discussed at large hereafter. After the description of weapons is finished, the different modes of warring, marching, and treating are gone into, and the political conduct of the king is described at length. No undue preference is given to any peculiar subject in particular, and this, if no other proof had been forthcoming, speaks for the genuineness of the work.

It is hardly imaginable that a work, which contains so many important revelations about the ancient state of the civil and military administration of India, and which is, as we have seen, often quoted by works of undisputed antiquity and genuineness—quoted too in a manner which precludes forgery, as the quotations are seldom quite literal—should have been written for the sole object of braggadocio, in order to prove to Europeans the mental superiority of the ancient Hindus by ascribing to them the original invention and manufacture both of gunpowder and firearms, and that the very object of the forgery, its *raison d'être*, should have been frustrated afterwards by keeping the work so zealously secret that except to a few initiated pandits, it was totally unknown to the public!

On the other hand would it not be a subject worthy of investigation for those who doubt the authenticity of the Śukranīti to prove its spuriousness, and to refute the statements brought forward in favor of its genuineness? Mere assertions do not possess any scientific value.

---

[81] Gunpowder and firearms are incidentally mentioned also in other parts of the Sukranīti: but in this chapter both are described fully.

The language is simple, terse and antiquated, and in many instances the age of the work manifests itself in this respect. The Śukranīti contains also a large number of half verses and this is another circumstance speaking for its antiquity. In some places it contradicts the precepts of Manu, and as it is not likely that any Hindu would dare to oppose that most venerated law book, we may conclude that the compilation of our work is anterior to or at least contemporary with our revision of Manu's Dharmaśāstra.

Śukra is regarded as the preceptor of the Demons, and though this tradition should be received *cum grano salis*, nevertheless the work written by or ascribed to him may have been regarded as the special law book of the warriors or Kṣatriyas. It was also for this reason originally not much patronised by the Brahmans, but now it is held in great respect by them.[82]

CHAPTER III.

ON THE USE OF GUNPOWDER AND FIREARMS IN GENERAL.

No invention has, within the last five hundred years, been so influential in shaping the destinies of nations as the introduction of gunpowder and of firearms into warfare. The fate of whole realms depended, and depends to a certain extent even now, on the proficiency attained by the comba-

---

[82] A copy of the Śukranīti was bought for the Government MSS. Library by my predecessor Mr. Śeṣagiri Śāstrī as far back as 1871, but as long as I could consult only this copy, I could not well attempt to print it. Since that time I have received three more Manuscripts of this work from other parts of the country, which, though coming from different places and being written in different characters, are in very close agreement. A printed specimen published a few years ago by H.H. the Holkar has also come into my hands, and though it is a print abounding with mistakes, it serves me as another Manuscript.

The Śukranīti is now very scarce, and its owners do not like to part with it. I have therefore been obliged to get two MSS. copied, as I could not obtain the originals.

tants in the manufacture of better gunpowder or of projectile weapons of superior quality.

When missiles despatched from projectile weapons by means of gunpowder easily penetrated the knights clad in their strongest suit of armour, while the persons who used those arms were quite beyond the reach of their physically perhaps stronger foes, no wonder that armour was discarded in course of time, and the mediæval knight, who had hitherto without much difficulty maintained his supremacy single-handed against a multitude, found his former superiority gone, and disappeared gradually from the scene. Fortresses, which, before the invention of gunpowder, had been regarded as impregnable, lost their reputation as safe strongholds, and new schemes and practices had to be devised to obviate the difficulties of the altered situation.

Slight improvements in the construction or manipulation of firearms produced often most important alterations in the political history of the world. Frederick the Great is said to have owed in his earlier campaigns many of his victories to the quicker mode of loading adopted by the Prussian army; and it is not so long ago that we ourselves have witnessed a rearrangement of the map of Europe, partly effected by means of superior weapons being used by one nation against another. It is therefore natural that a general interest should be more or less taken in all important advances made in this subject, which, if well studied and applied, provides a nation with the means of ensuring its freedom, independence, and supremacy, so long as actual strength is regarded as the only recognized claim to independent political existence.

The invention of gunpowder has been ascribed to different individuals belonging to different countries, and as the question as to its authorship and antiquity is still an open one, we shall discuss this mooted point and shall endeavour to prove that the oldest documents mentioning and describing gunpowder are found in India and written in Sanskrit, and that the use of gunpowder and its application to the discharge of missiles from projectile weapons was a well known fact in ancient India, corroborating so far the opinion of those who always pointed out India as the original seat of its invention. The question whether China received the knowledge of gunpowder from India, or *vice versâ*, cannot be touched here, as there do not exist any trustworthy documents bearing on this question. No Chinese work on this question can, with respect to antiquity, be compared with the Śukranīti, so that even if the Chinese should have independently invented gunpowder, the claim as to priority of invention will certainly remain with India.

A Franciscan monk, Berthold Schwarz, whose real name was Constantin Ancklitzen or Anklitz, is generally, especially in Germany, credited with the invention of gunpowder, which, according to tradition, was made at Freiburg in the Breisgau about the year 1330. No doubt Black Barthel, *der schwarze Barthel*, as he was popularly called, dabbled in alchemy and was very fond of chemical experiments, during one of which he was blown up and nearly killed by an explosion of a mortar he was experimenting upon. Eventually he was accused of practising magic and necromancy and sent to prison. A grateful posterity erected in his honour a statue on the spot where the Franciscan Convent of Freiburg had once stood; an honour which he may have richly deserved for many reasons, but surely not for being the original inventor of gunpowder.

Many years previously to Berthold Schwarz, another Franciscan monk, Roger Bacon (1214–94), the Doctor Mirabilis of Oxford, had already pointed out the peculiar qualities of saltpetre, as exemplified in the action of gunpowder. Like every chemical scholar in those times he became an object of clerical suspicion, was incarcerated by his superiors on the plea of practising forbidden magic and though for a time released by Pope Clement IV, he was again imprisoned under Pope Nicholas III. Bacon suggests that gunpowder should be used in war, as it would supply a powerful means for the destruction of hostile armies. He notices particularly the thunderlike noise and lightninglike flash at the time of its explosion; its application to crackers and fireworks is a subject, he was well acquainted with. He states in his book on the secret works of art and nature two of the principal ingredients which compose gunpowder—saltpetre and sulphur—but not wishing, according to the mysterious inclination of those days, to make the secret known, he uses in his prescription the obscure expression *lura nope cum ubre*, which has been later ingeniously found out to stand for *carbonum pulvere.*[83]

It is now generally supposed that Roger Bacon learnt the secret of the manufacture of gunpowder while he was travelling in Spain, where it was pretty well known among the Moors, who were not only the most learned nation at that period, but who, through religious and national tradition were intimately connected with their more eastern co-religionists and compatriots. An Arabic treatise on gunpowder written in 1249 is up to this day preserved in the Library of the Royal Escurial.

In the National Library at Paris is preserved a work ascribed to one Marcus Graecus. It was published at Paris in 1806 as *Liber ignium ad comburendos hostes, auctore Marco Graeco*. About the nationality and the life of this Marcus Graecus nothing is known for certain. According to some he lived in the 9th, according to others in the 13th

[83] "Sed tamen salis petrae, *lura nope cum ubre* et sulphuris, et sic facies tonitrum et coruscationem, si scias artificium," in Roger Bacon's work "*De secretis operibus Artis et Naturae et de nullitate magiae.*" At another place he alludes to fireworks: "Ex hoc ludicro puerili quod fit in multis mundi partibus scilicet ut instrumento facto ad quantitatem pollicis humani ex hoc violentia salis qui salpetrae vocatur tam horribilis sonus nascitur in ruptura tam modicae pergamenae quod fortis tonitru rugitum et coruscationem maximam sui luminis jubar excedit."

century. The accuracy of the name is even doubtful, as he is also called Marcus Gracchus instead of Graecus. If the latter appellation be the more correct one, it might perhaps be surmised that the work was originally written in Greek. Saltpetre occurs three times in his book, as *sal petrosum; lapis qui dicitur petra salis*, and as *sal petrum.* [84] According to Marcus Graecus the composition of gunpowder is two parts of charcoal, one part of sulphur, and six parts of saltpetre.

Towards the end of the seventh century the architect Kallinikos of Heliopolis, when Constantinople was besieged by the Arabs in 668, manufactured big tubes made of iron or of other metals, formed like big beasts with gaping jaws, out of which were thrown iron, stones and combustibles. In consequence of the havoc caused by these projectiles the siege of the city was raised. The Greeks kept, it is said, the secret of the composition for four centuries, when it was betrayed to the Saracens, who availed themselves of it during the crusades at Jerusalem and also at Damietta. If the ingredients are rightly mentioned, *e.g.*, by the Byzantine princess, Anna Komnena, who wrote the history of her father Alexios, they consisted only of resin, oil, and sulphur, and not of saltpetre. As Kallinikos hailed from Heliopolis, the place otherwise known as Baalbec, and as the Greek fire seems to have been a liquid, the most important ingredient of which was naphtha, which was well known to, and was much made use of by the Eastern nations,—as it is found near Baku on the Caspian Sea, (where the gas, as it escapes from fissures in the earth in the neighbourhood of the oilsprings, has been burning unintermittedly for centuries and is worshipped by Parsees,) in the island of Tchelekin on the other side of the Caspian Sea opposite to Baku, in Mesopotamia, in Kurdistan, in North India, and in China—it is probable that Kallinikos only introduced this powerful com-

[84] *See* John Beckmann's History of Inventions and Discoveries under the article "*Saltpetre, Gunpowder, Aqua fortis.*"

bustible into Western warfare, and that it was before his time employed in the East. At all events it was a most powerful preparation for the destruction of the enemy, and the terror it spread among the troops of Louis IX before Damietta is graphically described by contemporaries. It seems to have even been used in European wars, for, according to Père Daniel, the king Philip Augustus of France had brought home some of it from Acre, and used it at the siege of Dieppe against the English ships there at anchor.[85] It is said that Napoleon the Great became acquainted with the real composition of the Greek fire, but that he pronounced it inapplicable; one of the chief reasons for his decision being probably the fluid state of the combustible.

There exists an old tradition, according to which the Arabs possessed at an early date a knowledge of the manufacture of gunpowder, and that they obtained it originally from India, with which country they had an active commercial intercourse. They are even said to have improved on the original manufacture. That the Arabs received their earliest gunpowder supplies from India, and that this country was the original seat of its invention was very strongly urged so early as the end of the last century by M. Langlès in a paper read in the French Institute in 1798. This opinion is also upheld by Johann Beckmann (1739–1811), whose well known "History of Inventions and Discoveries" (*Beiträge zur Geschichte der Erfindungen*) has passed through many English editions. He says there: "In a word, I am more than ever inclined to accede to the opinion of those who believe that gunpowder was invented in India, and brought by the Saracens from Africa to the Europeans; who, however, improved the preparation of it, and found out different ways of employing it in war, as well as small arms and cannons."

---

[85] *See* Projectile Weapons of War and Explosive Compounds; by J. Scoffern, M.B., third edition, London, 1858, pp. 50–60.

Having discussed so far the question as to the invention of gunpowder, we now turn to its application in war by means of projectile weapons. The first country in Europe where such projectile weapons were used was Spain. They are mentioned by Arabian writers as far back as 1312, and were used in 1323 at the siege of Baza. The French seem to have employed them since 1338 at first for dismantling castles and fortifications only, and not in the battle field as Edward III of England is said to have done in 1346 at Crecy. The French writers seem to have been indignant at the employment of such destructive arms against human beings, for one of them says: "On ne faisoit point encore usage en France en 1347 de cette arme terrible contre les hommes; les François s'en étoient bien servis en 1338, pour l'attaque de quelques chateaux, mais ils rougissoient de l'employer contre leurs semblables. Les Anglois, moins humains, sans doute, nous devancèrent et s'en servirent à la célèbre bataille de Creci, qui eut lieu entre les troupes du roi d'Angleterre, Edouard III, qui fut si méchant, si perfide, qui donna tant de fil à retordre à Philippe de Valois, et aux troupes de ce dernier; et ce fut en majeure partie à la frayeur et à la confusion qu'occasionnèrent les canons, dont les Anglois se servoient pour la première fois, qu'ils avoient postés sur une colline proche le village de Creci, que les François durent leur déroute."[86] These projectile weapons were formed like tubes and were therefore called *cannons* from *canna*, a reed. In German they were known as *Rohr*, which word has the same meaning. The small firearms were originally without a stock, and as they were very heavy, they used to be placed on a fork when they were discharged. The *arquebuse* with a wheel was first used by Emperor Charles V and Pope Leo X in the year 1521 at the siege of Parma against Francis I, King of France.

---

[86] *See* Projectile Weapons of War, p. 117.—In the Library of Christ Church, Oxford, is preserved in a beautifully illuminated Manuscript, which dates from 1336, and which has been in the possession of Edward III, the picture of an armour-clad warrior, who fires a bottle-shaped cannon.

The same Martin Bellay who states this fact, further informs us that the German horse or *Reiter* were the first, who were armed with pistols, and that those troopers were thence called pistoliers. *Musket* is a still later weapon. It has got its name from the French *mouchet* (Latin *muschetus*, sparrow hawk).[87] The Duke of Alva is reported to have first used them in the Netherlands.

The gun was originally fired by the simple application of a lighted match. The clumsiness and uncertainty of this procedure especially during storms and rains suggested improvements. At first a cock was added to give security to the hand, afterwards a firestone was inserted into this cock and a small wheel was fastened to the barrel. The wheel lock is said to have been invented in 1517 at Nürnberg in Bavaria. The firestone first used was not the flint which was employed later, but the pyrites or marcasite. The match was nevertheless not altogether discarded, as the stone often missed fire, and it was retained together with the wheel. Flint locks were of a far later origin. They were first used in 1687 by the Brunswickers, and they were introduced into England under William III during the years 1692-93. These continued improvements, to which we may add the modern percussion lock, the needle-gun, and the breech-loader, were mainly necessitated by the perilous and defenceless position a soldier was in as soon as he had discharged his gun against an enemy, who chose this moment as convenient to attack him. The greater the rapidity in loading, the greater is the efficiency of the fireweapon.

If we now turn our attention from the West to the East we find that powder and firearms seem to have been much earlier used in the latter than in the former.

It is recorded that in the battle near Delhi fought between Tamerlane and Sultan Mahmud, the latter opposed his

---

[87] According to others it was invented at the end of the fifteenth century by one Moketta of Velletri, after whom it is said to have been named.

enemy with 10,000 horsemen, 40,000 men on foot, and a great number of elephants clad in armour. On the top of those elephants were big howdahs from which the sharpshooters flung fireworks and rockets on the troops of Timur; and on the sides of those elephants marched "des jetteurs de pots à feu et de poix enflamée ainsi que des fusées volantes pointées de fer, qui donnent plusieurs coups de suite dans le lieu où ils tombent."[88] According to Clavigo, Timur was beaten in the first engagement through those 50 mailed elephants, but on the following day Timur took many camels and loaded them with dry grass placing them in front of the elephants. When the battle began, he caused the grass to be set on fire and when the elephants saw the burning straw upon the camels, they fled."[89] When attacking Bhatnīr, Timur's troops were received in a similar manner for "the besieged cast down in showers arrows and stones and fireworks upon the heads of the assailants."[90]

According to Ferishṭa, Hulaku Khan, the founder of the Mogol Empire in Western Asia, sent in 1258 an ambassador to the King of Delhi, and when the ambassador was approaching he was received by the vezir of the king with a great retinue, and among the splendid sights were 3,000 fire cars. About the same time we are informed that in the wars between the Chinese and the Mogol invaders a kind of fire-arms was used. It seems to have been like a rocket. It was called impetuous *fire dart*. "A nest of grains—case of chick peas—was introduced into a long tube of bamboo, which, on being ignited, darted forth a violent flame, and instantly the charge was projected with a noise like that of a *pao*, which

---

88 *See* Histoire de Timur-bec, par Cherifeddin Ali d'Yezd, traduite par le feu M. Petits de la Croix. 1723, III, p. 94.

89 *See* Narrative of the Embassy of Ruy Gonzalez de Clavijo to the Court of Timur at Samarcand. London, 1859, p. 153.

90 *See* Malfūzāt-i-Tīmūrī in Sir H. M. Elliot's Histories of India, III, 424.

was heard at about the distance of 150 paces."[91] Deguignes says that the Mogols used in 1275 a similar weapon against the Chinese: "Les Chinois reprirent Tchangtcheou; et Tchang-chi-kiai avec un grand nombre de barques qu'il avait ramassées, s'approcha pour combattre les Mogols. Mais At-chou avec des flèches enflammées, y fit mettre le feu, et les troupes Chinoises, après une vive résistance, se précipitèrent dans le fleuve."[92] At another place Deguignes under the year 917 says that the Kitans[93] carried with them a combustible which they had received from the King of Ou, and that this fluid burnt even under water.[94] Arabian reports inform us that the Arabs used in India *Átish-bāzī*, like those employed by the Greeks and Persians. Ferishta tells us that in the battle which Mahmud of Ghazna fought near Peshawar with Ānandapāl in 1,008 cannon (*top*) and muskets (*tufang*) were used by Mahmud.[95] Colonel Tod says in his Annals of Rajasthan: "We have, in the poems of the Hindu poet Chand, frequent indistinct notices of fire-arms, especially the *nalgola*, or tube ball; but whether discharged by percussion or the expansive force of gunpowder is dubious. The poet

---

[91] *See* On the early use of Gunpowder in India; in "The History of India" the posthumous papers of the late Sir H. M. Elliot, K.C.B., edited by Professor John Dawson, vol. VI., p. 460. Ibidem in note 2 is a quotation from Père Gaubil's "Historie de Gentchiscan," p. 69. Les Mangous se servirent alors de *pao* (ou canons) à feu. On avait dans la ville des *pao* à feu . . . Je n'ai pas osé traduire par *canon*, les charactères *pao*, et *ho pao*, un de ces caractères a à côté le charactère *ché*, *pierre*, et c'était une machine à lancer des pierres. L'autre charactère est joint au charactère *ho*, *feu*, et je ne sais pas bien si c'était un canon comme les nôtres. De même, je n'oserais assurer que les boulets dont il est parlé se jetaient comme on fait aujourd'-hui.

[92] *See* "Histoire générale des Huns, par M. Deguignes, III, 162.

[93] On the Khitans see my book "Der Presbyter Johannes in Sage und Geschichte," pp. 121-126.

[94] *See* Deguignes, II, p. 61: "Ils (les Khitans) apportoient avec eux une matière inflammable, dont le Roi de Ou leur avoit donné la connoissance, c'était une matière grasse qui s'enflammoit et qui brûloit au milieu des eaux.

[95] *See* The History of India, edited from Sir H. M. Elliot's papers by Prof. John Dowson, VI, 219 and 454.

also repeatedly speaks of "the volcano of the field," giving to understand great guns; but these may be interpolations, though I would not check a full investigation of so curious a subject by raising a doubt." [96] Muhammed Kāsim used such a machine or *manjanīk* when besieging in A.H. 93 (A.D. 711–12) the port of Daibal. The first thing done with this machine was to shoot down from the top of the high pagoda a long pole surmounted with a red cloth.[97] The prophet Muhammed is also credited with having used the *manjanīk* when besieging Tāif in the ninth year of the Hegira, and according to Ibn Kotaibah the projectile weapon in question was already used by Jazynah, the second King of Hyrah, whose date is fixed about the year 200 A.D.[98]

Passing over the statements of Dio Cassius and Johannes Antiochenus, that the Roman Emperor Caligula had machines from which stones were thrown among thunder and lightning, we come to the statement of Flavius Philostratos, who lived at the court of the Emperors Septimius Severus, and Caracalla. In his history of Apollonios of Tyana, he mentions, that when that extraordinary man was travelling in India, he had among other things learnt the real reason why Alexander the Great desisted from attacking the Oxydracae. "These truly wise men dwell between the rivers Hyphasis and Ganges; their country Alexander never entered, deterred not by fear of the inhabitants, but, as I suppose, by religious motives, for had he passed the Hyphasis, he might, doubtless, have made himself master of all the country round them; but their cities he never could have taken, though he had led a thousand as brave as Achilles, or three thousand such as Ajax, to the assault; for they come not out to the field to fight those who attack them, but these holy men, beloved by the gods, overthrew their enemies with tempests and thunderbolts shot from their walls. It is said that the Egyptian

[96] *See* Annals of Rājasthan, I, 310.

[97] *See* Elliot's Posthumous Papers, VI, 462. [98] *Ibidem*, p. 461.

Hercules and Bacchus, when they overran India, invaded this country also, and having prepared warlike engines, attempted to conquer them; they in the meanwhile made no show of resistance, appearing perfectly quiet and secure, but upon the enemy's near approach they were repulsed with storms of lightning and thunderbolts hurled upon them from above." In the apocryphal letter which Alexander is said to have written to Aristotle, he describes the frightful dangers to which his army were exposed in India, when the enemies hurled upon them flaming thunderbolts.[99]

Firdusi ascribed to Alexander this expedient when opposed by Porus. While Sikander, according to the author of the Shah-Nama, was marching against Porus (Fur) his troops became so frightened when they perceived the numbers of elephants which Porus was sending against them that Alexander consulted his ministers how to counteract this foe. Their advice was to manufacture an iron man and an iron horse, place the former on the latter, fix the horse on wheels, fill them both with naphtha and propel them towards the elephants, where they would explode with great havoc.

Such a stratagem is ascribed by the Franciscan monk Johannes de Plano Carpini to Prester John when he was fighting against the Tatars. In my monograph on Prester John I have pointed out to what special event it may probably refer.[100]

---

[99] *See* Philostratos Τὰ εἰς τὸν Τυανέα Ἀπολλώνιον. The words used by Philostratos are *βρονταὶ κάτω στρεφόμεναι* (II, 14), and *ἐμβροντηθέντας αὐτοὺς ὑπὸ τῶν σοφῶν* (III, 3).—Compare Projectile Weapons of War, pp. 83 and 84.

[100] *See* Der Presbyter Johannes in Sage und Geschichte, pp. 93 and 94. "Johannes Presbyter venit contra eos (Tataros) exercitu congregato, et faciens imagines hominum cupreas in sellis posuit supra equos, ponens ignem interius, et posuit homines cum follibus post imagines cupreas supra equos; et cum multis imaginibus et equis taliter praeparatis venerunt contra praedictos Tartaros ad pugnam; et cum ad locum prœlii pervenissent, istos equos unum juxta alium praemiserunt, viri autem qui erant retro, posuerunt nescio quid ignem qui erat in praedictis imaginibus et cum follibus fortiter sufflaverunt; unde factum est quod ex igne graeco homines comburebantur et equi, et ex fumo aer est denigratus."

We read in the extracts remaining from the work of Ktesias[101] on India, that an oil was prepared from a big worm, which lived in the deep bed of the river Indus. This animal had two big tusks (jaws? *branchiæ*), slept during the day in the muddy sands of the banks of the rivers, which it left at night in search of food, seizing big animals, which it devoured. According to C. Plinius Secundus this worm catches even elephants.[102] When such an animal has been caught—which is generally done by binding a sheep or a goat to a strong pole—it is kept suspended in the sun for thirty days, that the oil may drip from it, and this oil was collected in earthen pots. Each worm supplied a quantity equal to ten measures of oil. This was sent to the king in sealed jars. The oil had the power to ignite every thing and was for this reason used especially at sieges. Jars filled with this material were thrown into besieged towns and whatever they touched ignited as soon as they broke. Nothing but rubbish and sweepings could extinguish the flame, when once ignited. Neither man, nor animal, nor anything could

---

101 *See* Photii Myriobiblon, 1653, p. 153-156.

Ὅτι ἐν τῷ ποταμῷ τῶν Ἰνδῶν σκώληξ γίνεται, τὸ μὲν εἶδος οἷόν περ ἐν ταῖς συκαῖς εἴωθε γίνεσθαι, τὸ δὲ μῆκος, πήχεων ἑπτὰ τοὺς μείζους δὲ καὶ ἐλάττους. τὸ δὲ πάχος δεκαετέα παῖδα μόλις φασὶ ταῖς χερσὶ περιβαλεῖν. ἔχουσι δὲ ὀδόντας δύο, ἕνα ἄνω καὶ ἕνα κάτω· καὶ ὅ,τι ἂν λάβωσι τοῖς ὀδοῦσι, κατεσθίουσι. καὶ τὴν μὲν ἡμέραν ἐν τῇ ἰλύϊ τοῦ ποταμοῦ διαιτῶνται, τῇ δὲ νυκτὶ ἐξέρχον. καὶ τούτων ὃς ἂν εὐτύχῃ τινὶ ἐν τῇ γῇ, βοῒ ἢ καμήλῳ, καὶ δάκῃ συλλαβὼν ἕλκει εἰς τὸν ποταμὸν, καὶ πάντα κατεσθίει πλὴν τὰς κοιλίας. ἀγρούε δὲ ἀγκίστρῳ μεγάλῳ, ἔριφον ἢ ἄρνα ἐνδησάντων τῷ ἀγκίστρῳ, καὶ ἁλύσεται σιδηραῖς ἐναρμοσάντων. ἀγρούσαντες δὲ τριάκοντα ἡμέρας κρεμῶσιν αὐτον. καὶ ἀγγεῖα ὑποτιθέασι. καὶ ῥεῖ ἐξ αὐτοῦ, ὅσον δέκα κοτύλας ἀττικὰς τὸ πλῆθος. ὅσαν δὲ παρέλθωσιν αἱ τριάκοντα ἡμέραι, ἀποῤῥίπτουσι τὸν σκώληκα. καὶ τὸ ἔλαιον ἀσφαλισάμενοι, ἄγουσι τῷ βασιλεῖ μόνῳ τῶν Ἰνδῶν. ἄλλῳ δὲ οὐκ ἔξεστιν ἐξ αὐτοῦ ἔχειν. τοῦτο τὸ ἔλαιον, ἐφ' ὃ ἂν ἐπιχυθῇ, ἀνάπτει· καὶ καταφλέγει ξύλα καὶ ζῶα. καὶ ἄλλως οὐ σβέννυτι εἰ μὴ πηλῷ πολλῷ τε καὶ παχεῖ.

102 *See* Caii Plinii Secundi *Historiæ Naturalis*, Libr. IX, 17 : "In eodem (Gange flumine) esse Statius Sebosus haud medico miraculo affert, vermes branchiis binis, sex cubitorum, cæruleos, qui nomen a facie traxerunt. His tantas esse vires, ut elephantos ad potum venientes, mordicus comprehensa manu eorum abstrahant." Just previously Plinius had spoken of the Delphinus Gangeticus (platanista).

withstand this terrific combustible. Philostratos confirmed these statements. According to him this worm-like insect lives in the Hyphasis, and the flame caused by the fire can only be subdued by being entirely covered with dust. The king is the sole owner of all these animals. Ktesias, Aelianos, and Philostratos, all three agree in the name of this *worm*, which they call Skolex (σκώληξ). Lassen scorns the possibility of such a worm being in existence, and ascribes the whole description to the imaginative tendency so prevailing in the mind of Oriental nations. The late Professor H. H. Wilson takes a more practical view of the case, by identifying the worm in question with the Indian alligator, and remembering that the oil and the skin of the alligator were considered in ancient times to possess most wonderful qualities, and that the greater part of the other description tallies with the outward appearance and natural habits of the alligator. Wilson seems to have fixed on the right animal.[103] Nevertheless so far as the name σκώληξ is concerned nobody so far as I know has tried to explain it. An animal of seven cubits in length, and of a breadth in proportion to its size, could hardly have been called a *worm*, unless the original name of the beast in question resembled the Greek word *Skolex.* The word represented by the Greek word Skolex is no doubt the Sanskrit term *culukī*, *cullakī* (with the variations *ulupin* or *culumpin*). *Culukin* is derived from *culuka*, mire, it is therefore an animal which likes to lie or to live in mud. The cullakī is described in Sanskrit works as somewhat similar to the *Śiśumāra*, which is identified with the Delphinus Gange-

[103] *See* Indische Alterthumskunde von Christian Lassen, II, pp. 641 and 642. "Unter diesen Erzeugnissen der überschwänglichen Einbildungskraft der Inder möge hier noch besonders gedacht werden, des aus im Indus lebenden Würmern gewonnenen Oeles, welches die Eigenschaft besessen haben soll, alles anzuzünden und zu der Ansicht verleitet hat, das die alten Inder Feuerwaffen gekannt hätten. Diese Nachricht muss im Gegentheil gebraucht werden, um zu beweisen, dass schon zur Zeit des Ktesias dichterische Vorstellungen, welche den Indern eigenthümlich sind, den Persern bekannt geworden waren." Compare also Elliot's History of India, VI, pp. 478–80.

ticus, though its name denotes a *childkiller*. The cullakī is therefore a large aquatic animal, which because it lives principally in water, is called a fish ; and as the crocodile prefers as its place of abode the muddy banks of a river, the name *cullakī* applies most appropriately to it.[104]

It is a peculiar coincidence that in Telugu an iguana is called *uḍumu*, and the lizard is generally called *uḍumupille* or young iguana; the Tamil name of the same animal is *uḍumbu*.

The identity is thus clearly established between the Greek word *skolex* (as the Greeks had no nearer sound than *sk* to resemble the palatal *c*), the Sanskrit words *culukī* (cullakī, culumpī, and ulupī), and the Dravidian *uḍumbu* and *uḍumu*.

On the west coast of India oil is even now obtained from big fish by letting their carcasses lie in the sun and allowing the oil thus to ooze out, which process creates all the while an unbearable stench. With respect to the quantity of oil gained out of a fish like a porpoise and of a crocodile, the superiority rests doubtless with the former, though a well-fed and plump gavial possesses no doubt likewise a considerable amount of oily substance.[105]

The iguana resembles in its shape a crocodile, and both being named in the Dravidian languages and in Sanskrit by the word *culumpī* alias *uḍumbu*, this term applies in the former languages to the smaller and in Sanskrit to the larger animal. The Sanskrit word *musalī* and the Tamil *mudalai* are also identical in origin, but they differ in so far that *musalī*

---

[104] The author of the Śabdaratnāvali explains it by *Śiśumārākṛtimatsya*, *i.e.*, a fish which resembles the porpoise; and in Hemacandra's Anekārtha-saṅgraha we read *cullakī kuṇḍikā bhede śiśumāre kulāntare ;* Viśvaprakāśa and Medinīkara have nearly the same explanation: *Culukī* (*cullakī*) *śiśumārepi kuṇḍibhede kalāntare*, *i.e.*, culukī is a pot; a porpoise (and) a kind of race.

[105] The oil of the crocodile is mentioned in Indian Medical Works, and it is in the list of Dr. Forbes Watson included among the commercial products of India.

denotes a house lizard and *mudalai* a crocodile. In fact the Sanskrit *musalī* and *culumpin* (*culukī*) correspond according to their meaning to the Tamil *uḍumbu* and *mudalai*. The inference to be drawn from this fact is obvious.

The *culukin* is in Sanskrit only a large sized animal; a worm, especially an earth-worm, is called a *kiñculuka* or *kiñculaka* or kiñcilaka, *i.e.*, a little culuka.

No doubt the description of Ktesias is in many respects inaccurate, but I hope to have been able to trace the thread of truth which runs through it.

As oil, especially boiling oil, is used in Indian warfare, the subject is of particular interest in this inquiry.

CHAPTER IV.

INDIA THE HOME OF GUNPOWDER AND FIREARMS.

In every inquiry which is conducted with the object of proving that a certain invention has been made in any particular country it is of the utmost importance to show that so far as the necessary constituents of the object invented are concerned, all these could be found in the country credited with such invention.

The ordinary components of gunpowder, are saltpetre, sulphur, and charcoal.

1. It is now generally admitted that the *nitrum* which occurs in the writings of the ancients was not saltpetre, but *natron*, *i.e.*, sodium carbonate; the latter word is nowhere extant in Greek or Roman literature, though the words *nitrum* and *natron* are no doubt in their origin identical.

The word *neter* occurs twice in the Bible. It is described as an alkali, which was used as soap: "For though thou wash thee with nitre, and take thee much sope, yet thine iniquity is marked before me, saith the Lord God" (Jerem. ii. 22); and "As he that taketh away a garment in cold weather, and as vinegar upon nitre, so is he that singeth songs to an heavy heart." (Proverbs. xv. 22.)

Herodotos mentions nitrum as litron (*λίτρον*) in his description of the embalming of dead bodies as practised in Egypt.[106] Pliny repeatedly speaks of nitrum, and Galen [107] records that it was burnt to strengthen its qualities. This would have had no effect if applied to salpetre. There is no doubt that had the ancients known saltpetre, its oxydizing properties would soon have been discovered by them, which is the most important step towards the invention of gunpowder.

The word *natron* was introduced into Europe from the East by some European scholars who had been travelling there about the middle of the sixteenth century and who had thus become acquainted with this salt; [108] and though the word natron was originally used there for denoting saltpetre, its other form *nitrum* has been since assigned it; however, as we have seen, the nitrum of the ancients is quite different from our nitre, which is saltpetre (*potassium nitrate*).

Native saltpetre, *i.e.*, saltpetre produced by entirely natural processes is very scarce, so much so that the inventor of *nickel*, Freiherr Axel Friedrich von Cronstedt (1722–65) was unacquainted with it. It is found especially in India, Egypt, and in some parts of America. Since the introduction of gunpowder in European warfare saltpetre has been manufactured wherever native saltpetre could not be obtained in sufficient quantities. It was obtained, from the efflorescence on walls (sal murale) and other sources, this exudation,

---

[106] Herodotos, II. 86, *ταῦτα δὲ ποιήσαντες ταριχεύουσι λίτρῳ*, and 87, *τὰς δὲ σάρκας τὸ λίτρον κατατήκει.*

[107] Nitrum ustum proprius ad aphronitrum accedit, utpote ex ustione tenuius redditum (*λεπτομερέστερον*). Ceterum nitro usto simul et non usto . . . in talibus morbis uti consuevimus (*νίτρῳ δὲ κεκαυμένῳ τε καὶ ἀκαύστῳ καὶ ἡμεῖς ἐπὶ τοιούτων χρώμεθα.* Galenus, *De Simplic. Med. Facult.* IX. Dioscurides says also that nitrum was commonly burnt. Compare Beckmann's History of Inventions, II. 433.

[108] *See* J. Beckmann, History of Discoveries, under the head Saltpetre, Gunpowder, Aquafortis.

together with all the other artificial modes of producing saltpetre, became a perquisite of the sovereign, and this *saltpetre regale* grew in time into as obnoxious a burden to the people as the hunting regale. The saltpetre regale is first mentioned, as having been exercised in 1419 by Günther, Archbishop of Magdeburg.[109]

The little knowledge possessed by the ancients of chemical science, their utter ignorance of chemical analysis, accounts for their not improving, or rather for their not being able to improve the materials at their disposal and discovering the natural qualities of the different alkalis in their possession.

Throughout India saltpetre is found, and the Hindus are well acquainted with all its properties; it is even commonly prescribed as a medicine. India was famous for the exportation of saltpetre, and is still so. The Dutch, when in India, traded especially in this article.

In Bengal it is gathered in large masses wherever it effloresces on the soil, more particularly after the rainy season. In the Śukranīti saltpetre is called *suvarcilavaṇa*, well shining salt. The Dhanvantarinighaṇṭu describes saltpetre as a tonic, as a sonchal salt ; it is also called *tilakam* (black), *kṛṣṇalavaṇam* and *kālalavaṇam*. It is light, shiny, very hot in digestion and acid. It is good for indigestion, acute stomach ache, and constipation. It is a common medical prescription.[110]

2. Sulphur, the second ingredient of gunpowder, is also found in India, especially in Scinde ; it is, and was, largely

---

[109] *See* J. Beckmann, History of Discoveries, under the head Saltpetre, Gunpowder Aquafortis.

[110] *See* Dhanvantarinighaṇṭu, in the Description of Salts.

Suvarcalavaṇaproktam rucyakam hṛdyagandhakam
tilakam kṛṣṇalavaṇam tat kālalavaṇam smṛtam.
Laghu sauvarcalam pāke vīryoṣṇam viśadam kaṭu
gulmaśūlavibandhaghnam hṛdyam surabhilocanam.

Amarakoṣa, IX, 43. Sauvarcale'kṣarucake tilakam tatra mecake, and 110 sauvarcalam syāt rucakam.

imported into India from the East. It is well known and received its name from its smell, being called *gandha* or *gandhaka*, smell, or in this case as it has not a good smell, rather from its *stench*. Its quality differs with its color, according as it is white, red, yellow, or bluish. Though sulphur is a very important part of gunpowder, gunpowder is in some parts of India even prepared without it. Sulphur was always in great demand in India, and in medicine it is often made use of.[111]

3. *Charcoal* is the third component part of gunpowder. Its constitution varies necessarily with the plants which in the different countries are used in its manufacture. In Prussia the coal of the alder, limetree, poplar, elder, willow, hemp, and hazel is used for powder. The charcoal of willow trees is especially esteemed on account of its excellent qualities. In the Śukranīti the *arka* (*Calatropis giganteä*), the *snuhi*, *snuhī* or *snuh* (*Euphorbia neriifolia*), and the *Rasona* (*Allium sativum*) are given as the plants whose charcoal is best fitted for gunpowder.

The *arka*, gigantic swallow wort, is a common bush growing in great quantities all over the country. It has a very good fibre, and is regarded by the natives as possessing most powerful and useful qualities. If the arka is used with discretion when iron is being forged, it contributes greatly to the excellence of the Indian steel. It is applied against epilepsy, paralysis, dropsy, &c. Its milky juice is smeared on wounds. It is a common sight in India to see suffering people applying it. The root is also used against syphilis. Its charcoal is very light and much used for pyrotechnical

---

[111] Śveto raktaśca pītaśca nīlaśceti caturvidhaḥ
gandhako varṇato jñeyo bhinnabhinnaguṇāśrayaḥ ; *Rājanighaṇṭu.*

It is cleaned by being boiled with castor oil or goat's milk.

Gandhakam palamātram ca lohapatrāntare kṣipet
eraṇḍatailam sampūrya pacet śuddhirbhaviṣyati.
Athavā chāgadugdhena pacitam śuddhim āpnuyāt.

See Sadvaidyajīvana.

preparations, and its qualities in this respect are so well known that every school boy is acquainted with them and prepares his own powder and mixture with this plant. Its name in Tamil is *erukku,* in Malayalam *eruka,* in Telugu *jillēḍu*, in Bengali *akund,* and in Hindustani *mudar* or *ark.*

b. The *snuhī, snuh,* (triangular spurge, *kalli* in Malayālam, *pāśāṅ kalli* in Tamil, *bontajammuḍu* in Telugu, *narashy, seyard* in Hindustani and *narsy* in Bengali) grows like the arka in waste places all over the Indian Peninsula. The qualities of this plant for pyrotechnic displays are as well known as those of the Calatropis gigantea. Dried sticks of this plant are scarce. It is also widely used as a medicinal plant, externally against rheumatism, and internally as a purgative ; it is given to children against worms.[112]

c. The *rasona* is a kind of garlic ; the Marathi equivalent is *lasuna.* Its botanical name is *Allium sativum.*

The prescription for making gunpowder is, according to the Śukranīti, as follows : mix 5 parts of saltpetre with 1 part of sulphur and 1 part of charcoal. The charcoal is to be prepared from the arka, snuhi, and other similar plants in such a manner that during the process the plants are so covered that the smoke cannot escape. The charcoal thus obtained must be cleaned, reduced to powder, and the powder of the different charcoals is then to be mixed. After this has been done, the juice of the arka, snuhi, and rasona must be poured over the powder which is to be thoroughly mixed with this juice. This mixture is to be exposed and dried in the sun. It is then finally ground like sugar and the whole mixture thus obtained is gunpowder.[113]

---

[112] With respect to the *snuhi* there exists a Tamil proverb, reflecting on its leafless state and big growth. It runs as follows : " There is no leaf to contain a mustard seed ; but there is shade to shelter an elephant." (கடுகுசருட்ட இலையில்லை ; யானைதங்க இடமுண்டு).—*Compare also :* The Useful Plants of India, by Major Heber Drury, 1858, p. 100–102.

[113] *See* Chapter V, śl. 141, 142.

The proportion of saltpetre varies, as some take 4 or 6 parts instead of 5, but the quantities of sulphur and charcoal remain unaltered.[114] These two are the usual receipts. Nevertheless the mixture is often changed when the gunpowder is to be of a particular color or if it has to serve a special purpose. The three principal ingredients are mixed in different proportion, and realgar, opiment, graphite, vermilion, the powder of magnetic iron oxide, camphor, lac, indigo, and pine-gum are added to the compound according as they are required.[115]

It seems peculiar that powder should not have been mentioned in Sanskrit works, but this is not an isolated instance of the silence observed in them on matters of historical importance. It is most probable that the very common occurrence of gunpowder interfered with its being regarded as something extraordinary and worth mentioning. The actual mode of preparing the different sorts of gunpowder may on the other hand have been kept a secret in certain classes, and such a state of affairs coincides with the Indian system of caste. Explosive powder either used for rejoicings as fireworks or for discharging projectiles was known in India from the earliest period, and its preparation was never forgotten; but as India occupied in ancient times such an isolated position, it is not singular that the knowledge of this compound did not earlier extend to other countries. However wonderful the composition and however startling the detonating effect of powder may be to the uninitiated outsider, to those who have been familiar with them from their earliest youth all seems natural and intelligible. India is the land of fireworks; no festival is complete without them, and as the materials for their manufacture are all indigenous, and of easy access, there is no difficulty in gratifying such desires.

---

[114] *See* Chapter V, śl. 143.

[115] *See* Chapter V, śl. 146–148.

In an extract taken from the *Mujmalut Tawārīkh*—which was translated in 1126 from the Arabic, into which language it had been translated a century previously from a Sanskṛit original—we read: "that the Brahmans counselled Hāl to have an elephant made of clay and to place it in the van of his army, and that when the army of the king of Kashmir drew nigh, the elephant exploded, and the flames destroyed a great portion of the invading force. Here we have not only the simple act of explosion, but something very much like a fuze, to enable the explosion to occur at a particular time."[116]

Vaiśampāyana mentions among the things to be used against enemies *smoke-balls*, which contained most likely gunpowder, and which were according to the explanation proposed by his commentator made of gunpowder.[117]

The following stanza, which is taken from the Rājalakṣmīnārāyaṇahṛdaya, a part of the Atharvaṇarahasya, is no doubt a clear proof of the fact that the Hindus were familiar with gunpowder at a very remote period: "As the fire prepared by the combination of charcoal, sulphur, and other material depends upon the skill of its maker so also may thou, O! representative of knowledge (Lakṣmī), by the application of my faith manifest thyself quickly according to my wish."[118]

The Sanskrit word for gunpowder is *agnicūrṇa*, fire-powder, which is occasionally shortened into *cūrṇa*. The Dravidian languages have all one and the same word for medicine and gunpowder; in Tamil *marundu*, in Telugu *mandu*, in Kanarese *maddu*, and in Malayālam *maruna*.

---

[116] *See* the History of India of the late Sir H. M. Elliot, VI, 475; I, 107.
[117] *See* note 60.
[118] *See* Rājalakṣmīnārāyaṇahṛdaya:
Iṅgālagandhādipadārthayogāt
karturmanīṣānuguṇo yathāgniḥ
caitanyarūpe mama bhaktiyogāt
kāṅkṣānurūpam bhaja rūpam āśu.

Occasionally the word gun (*tupāki*) is prefixed to remove any doubt as to what powder is meant. In Malayālam, the word *veḍi*, which means explosion, is prefixed. The Chinese crackers are called by the Tamulians *Śīni veḍi*—Chinese crackers—to distinguish them from the Indian crackers. The word *marundu* is most probably derived from the Sanskrit past participle *mardita*, pounded, in the sense of different ingredients being pounded together, as a medicine powder. The meaning of gunpowder is then in a special sense derived from this general expression. The Dravidian equivalent of cūrṇa is *Śuṇṇāmbu* in Tamil, *Sunnamu* in Telugu, chalk.

From the subject of gunpowder we now turn to the weapon, to which it is applied, *i.e.*, to the firearms.

Two kinds of firearms are described in the Śukranīti, one is of small size and the other is of large size. The former is five spans long,[119] has at the breech a perpendicular and horizontal hole, and sights at the breech and muzzle end of the tube. Powder is placed in the vent, near which is a stone, which ignites the powder by being struck. Many dispense with this flint. The breech is well wooded and a ramrod compresses the powder and ball before the discharge. This small musket is carried by foot-soldiers.

A big gun has no wood at its breech; moves on a wedge in order to be directed towards the object to be shot at, and it is drawn on cars.

The distance which the shot travels depends upon the strength of the material from which the gun is made, upon the circumference of the hole, and the gun's compactness and size. The ball is either of iron or lead or of any other material. Some big balls have smaller ones inside. The gun itself is generally of iron, occasionally also, as we

[119] A span (vitasti) is the distance between the extended thumb and the little finger.

have seen in the Nītiprakāśikā, of stone. The gun is to be kept clean and must be always covered.[120]

The term used for gun *nālika* (*nalika*, *nālīka*) is derived from the word *nāla* (*nala*), a reed, a hollow tube, which is another form for its synonyms *naḍa*, *nāḍi*, or *nāḍī*; in the same way *nālika* corresponds to *nāḍika*. Considering that the guns were in ancient times made out of bamboo, and that some bamboo guns are still used in Burmah, the name appears both appropriate and original. That the idea of bamboo being the original material for guns was still in the mind of the author of the Śukranīti seems to be indicated by his calling the outside of the stock of a gun *bark* (tvak.)[121]

The gun is very seldom mentioned in Sanskrit writings, and even where it has been mentioned the meaning of those passages has been generally misunderstood. In all European Sanskrit dictionaries the word *nālika* or *nālīka* has been rendered as stalk, tube; arrow, dart, &c., but the third signification gun is not given; though it is one which is known to every learned Paṇḍit. At the outset every body can easily see that the meaning of arrow and of gun can be rightly applied to a reed; the arrow is a reed which is discharged as a missile, and a gun is a reed out of which missiles are shot.

In the ślokas 21 and 24 of our extract of the Śukranīti we read that a king should keep on a big war chariot two large guns, and in śl. 31 we are further informed that his beautiful iron chariot should be furnished with a couch, a swing, and among other things also with sundry arms and projectile weapons. This tallies with an account concerning the fortifications of Maṇipura, as described in Mr. J. Talboys Wheeler's "History of India:" On the outside of the city were a number of wagons bound together with chains, and in them

[120] *See* Śukranīti, Chapter V, śl. 135–39 and 149–151.
[121] *See* Śukranīti, Chapter V, śl. 139.

were placed fireworks and fire weapons, and men were always stationed there to keep guard." This statement is very important, and if substantiated would be of the greatest weight in this inquiry; but none of the Sanskrit Manuscripts of the Mahābhārata which I have searched contains this Śloka. However the above mentioned statement appears to rest on good authority, as the Śukranīti declares, that the wall of a fortress "is always guarded by sentinels, is provided with guns and other projectile weapons, and has many strong bastions with proper loop-holes and ditches."[122]

In the second stavaka of the Bhāratacampū composed by Anantabhaṭṭa, some three hundred years ago, we find the following simile: "The fierce warrior who killed his enemy with heaps of leaden balls, which emerge quickly from the gun lighted by a wick, is like the rainy season which killed the summer with hailstones which descend quickly from the rows of black clouds lighted by lightning."[123]

While the verse just quoted from the Bhāratacampū reveals an intimate knowledge of firearms, yet its apparent recentness may be alleged as an objection against its being produced as an authority for the existence of firearms in India at an early period. To obviate such further objections a śloka will now be given from an undoubted early poem, the Naiṣadha which describes the adventures of Nala and is generally ascribed to one Śrīharṣa, a Brahman, who must not be confounded with Śrīharṣa, the king of Kaśmīra. Its date goes back to the twelfth century, *i.e.*, before the introduction of firearms into Europe. The verses in question run as follows: "The two bows of Rati and Manmatha are

---

[122] *See* The History of India, Vol. I, pp. 405 & 422; and read Appendix.—*Compare* also Śukranīti I, 238 and 255.

238. Yāmikai rakṣito nityam nālikāstraiśca saṁyutaḥ
Subahudṛḍhagulmaśca sugavākṣapraṇālikaḥ.

[123] *See* Kālāmbudālinalikāt kṣaṇadīptivarttyām
sandhukṣitāt sapadi sadhvaninissaradbhiḥ;
varṣāśmasīsagulikānikaraiḥ kaṭhoraiḥ
gharmābhiyātim avadhīt ghanakālayodhaḥ.

certainly like her (Damayantī's) two brows, which are made for the conquest of the world, the two guns of those two (Rati and Manmatha) who wish to throw balls on you, are like her (Damayantī's) two elevated nostrils."[124] To leave no doubt that guns are meant here, the learned commentator Mallinātha explains *nālika* as the Droṇicāpa, the projectile weapon from which the *Droṇicāpaśara*, a dart or a ball is discharged, an expression, we have already noticed in Vaiśampāyana's Nītiprakāśikā.[125]

On the other hand it is doubtful whether the *aśani* missile, which was given by Indra to Arjuna and which made when discharged a noise like a thunder-cloud, alludes to firearms, as *von Bohlen* explains it.[126]

In the first book of the Śukranīti we find it stated that the royal watchmen, who are on duty about the palace, carry firearms. The Kāmandakīya, acknowledged as one of the earliest works on Nītiśāstra, says that "Confidential agents keeping near the king should rouse him by stratagems, gunfiring and other means, when he is indulging in drinking bouts, among women, or in gambling."[127] It seems from this statement that the practice of firing guns as signals

---

[124] *See* Naiṣadha, II, 28.

Dhanuṣī ratipañcabāṇayorudite viśvajayāya tadbhruvau
nalike na taduccanāsike tvayi nālīkavimuktikāmayoḥ.

Mallinātha explains the second line as follows: "Damayantyā uccanāsike unnatanāsāpuṭe tvayi nālīkānām *droṇicāpaśarāṇām* vimuktim kāmayate iti tathoktayostayośśīlakām abhikṣācaribhyo ṇa iti ṇa pratyayaḥ. Nalike *droṇicāpe* na kim iti kākūḥ pūrvavat utprekṣā.

[125] *See* p. 14.

[126] *See* Das alte Indien, mit besonderer Rücksicht auf Aegypten. Von Dr. P. von Bohlen, II, p. 66; *compare* Mahābhārata, Vanaparva, Indralokābhigamanaparva, I, 3, 4.

3. Evam sampūjito jiṣṇuruvāsa bhavane pituḥ
upaśikṣan mahāstrāṇi sa saṁhārāṇi pāṇḍavaḥ.
4. Cakrasya hastāt dayitam vajram astram ca dussaham
aśanīśca mahānādā meghavarhiṇalakṣaṇāḥ.

[127] *See* Kāmandakīya, V, 51.

Pānastrīdyūtagoṣṭhiṣu rājānam abhitaścarāḥ
bodhayeyuḥ pramādyantam upāyairnālikādibhiḥ.

All the MSS. I have consulted give nālika, and so do also the prints in Telugu and Grantha characters. The Calcutta edition has *nāḍika* which as

was in vogue among the ancient Hindus, if we can trust the evidence of one of the oldest Sanskrit writings.

In the preface to a Code of Gentoo Laws, or Ordinances of the Pundits, occurs the following passage: "It will no doubt strike the reader with wonder to find a prohibition of firearms in records of such unfathomable antiquity; and he will probably from hence renew the suspicion which has long been deemed absurd, that Alexander the Great did absolutely meet with some weapons of that kind in India as a passage in Quintus Curtius seems to ascertain. Gunpowder has been known in China, as well as in Hindustan, far beyond all periods of investigation. The word firearms is literally Sanskrit Agnee-aster, a weapon of fire; they describe the first species of it to have been a kind of dart or arrow tipt with fire and discharged upon the enemy from a bamboo. Among several extraordinary properties of this weapon, one was, that after it had taken its flight, it divided into several separate darts or streams of flame, each of which took effect, and which, when once kindled, could not be extinguished; but this kind of agnee-aster is now lost. Cannon in the Sanskrit idiom is called Shet-Agnee, or the weapon that kills a hundred men at once, from (Shete) a hundred, and (gheneh) to kill; and the Pooran Shasters, or Histories, ascribe the invention of these destructive engines to Beeshookerma, the artist who is related to have forged all the weapons for the war which was maintained in the Suttee Jogue between Dewtā and Ossoor

---

I explained on page 232 as *ḍ* and *l* are often interchanged, *ḍalayorabhedaḥ*, is another form for *nālika*, if not so it must be regarded as an altogether false reading. The word *nāḍika* (given in Böthlingk and Roth's Sanskrit Wörterbuch as nāḍikā) occurs nowhere else, and the only reference to it in the just now mentioned Sanskrit dictionary is this passage from the Kāmandakīya, and there even the meaning of the word is not positively stated, but it is merely suggested that it may be a gong (wohl., eine metallene Platte, an der die Stunden angeschlagen werden).

(or the good and bad spirits) for the space of one hundred years." [128]

And again we read in page 53 of the same work: "The Magistrate shall not make war with any deceitful machine, or with poisoned weapons, or with cannon and guns, or any other kind of firearms; nor shall he slay in war a person born an eunuch, or any person who putting his hands together supplicates for quarter, nor any person who has no means of escape, nor any man who is sitting down, nor any person who says, 'I am become of your party,' nor any man who is asleep, nor any man who is naked, nor any person who is not employed in war, nor any person who is come to see the battle, nor any person who is fighting with another, nor any person whose weapons are broken, nor any person who is wounded, nor any person who is fearful of the fight, nor any person who runs away from the battle."

As these passages are so often quoted without their origin being stated, it may at once be remarked that the prescription about the use of arms and the treatment of persons is a free translation from the seventh book of the institutes of Manu, vv. 90–93.

The important question at issue is, does this passage in Manu refer to firearms or not? In our opinion it certainly alludes to them, but still others prefer to apply it strictly to darts blazing with fire. The original words in Manu are:

Na kūṭair āyudhair hanyāt yudhyamāno raṇe ripūn
na karṇibhir nāpi digdhair *nāgnijvalitatejanaiḥ*.

"No one should strike in a combat his enemy with concealed weapons, nor with barbed arrows, nor with poisoned arrows, nor with darts kindled by fire." Kullūkabhaṭṭa, the latest

---

[128] *See* A Code of Gentoo Laws, or Ordinances of the Pundits, from a Persian translation, made from the original, written in the Shanscrit Language (by Nathaniel Brassey Halhed), London 1770, pp. LII, LIII, and 53.

commentator of Manu, favors by his explanation the opinion of those who take this passage in the sense "as darts blazing with fire."[129] But then the questions arise, whether Kullūkabhaṭṭa, who lived about four hundred years ago, expresses the *whole* meaning of the sentence, or whether Manu, though mentioning only ignited arrows, does not rather allude to firearms in general? The translation found in Dr. Monier Williams' Sanskṛit English Dictionary under *agnijvalitatejana* 'having a point hardened in fire' is quite beyond the mark.

The meaning of arrow (*śara, bāṇa*) is much wider than is generally supposed. It was, and became more so in time, the usual term for any missile, whether it had the shape of an arrow or not; in the same way as the word *Dhanu* signified in course of time every missile or weapon, so that the Dhanurveda, the knowledge of the bow comprised the knowledge of all other arms.

For instance, the shot out of a gun is called a *śara*, as we have seen when describing the nālika,[130] but it may be a ball and not an arrow. A rocket is generally styled a bāṇa (compare the Hindi term *bān*, a rocket); and *bāṇapaṭṭrai* in Tamil, or *bāṇapaṭra* in Telugu denotes a gunpowder or firework factory.

A comparison of the context of the Mānavadharmaśāstra with those of the Śukranīti and the Nītiprakāśikā makes it clear that Manu alludes to firearms. The Śukranīti runs in our extract as follows:—

277. A king, bearing in mind the six principles of policy and the designs of his enemy and his own, should always kill his enemy by fair and unfair fighting.

---

[129] *See* Kullūkabhatta to Manu, VII, 90. Kūṭānyāyudhāni bahiḥ kāṣṭhādimayāni antarguptaniśitaśastrāṇi; etaiḥ samare yudhyamānaḥ śatrum na hanyāt; nāpi karṇyakāraphalakairbāṇaiḥ; nāpi viṣāktaiḥ, nāpyagnidīptaphalakaiḥ.

[130] *See* note 25, *droṇicāpaśareriṇī*, discharging the missile of the Droṇicāpa.

278. When the king gladdens his soldiers on the march with a quarter extra pay, protects his body in the battle with a shield and armour;

279. has induced his soldiers to drink up to a state of intoxication, the strengthener of bravery, the soldier kills his enemy with a gun, swords, and other weapons.

280. A charioteer should be assailed by a lance, a person on a carriage or elephant by an arrow, an elephant by an elephant, a horse by a horse.

281. A carriage is to be opposed by a carriage, and a foot soldier also by a foot soldier, one person by another person, a weapon by a weapon, or a missile by a missile.

282. He should not kill a person who is alighted on the ground, nor one who is emasculated, nor one who has joined his hands as a supplicant, nor one who sits with dishevelled hair, nor one who says "I am thine."

Then follow beginning with 282 up to 284 the same exceptions as found in Manu, VII, 91—93, and specified in Halhed's Code.

The Śukranīti goes then on stating expressly:

286. These restrictions exist in fair but not in unfair fighting; to ensure the destruction of a powerful enemy there is no fighting equal to unfair fighting.

287. Unfair fighting was certainly observed by Rāma, Kṛṣṇa, Indra, and other gods; Bāli, Yavana, and Namuci were killed by unfair fighting.

We see thus that the Śukranīti is in direct opposition to the law code bearing Manu's name, and considering the estimation in which the latter was held, it can hardly be assumed that a member of the Brahmanic community—in which term I include all the three higher castes and the Śūdras within its pale—could have dared to compose it after the text of the Mānavadharmaśāstra had once been finally settled as it stands to this day.

The Nītiprakāśikā coincides entirely with Manu, VII, 89, and in the first half of the 90th śloka, but differs in the second half of the 90th and the first half of the 91st śloka, and then agrees again, but this difference in two lines is of the greatest importance for our subject.[131]

Manu, VII.	*Nītiprakāśikā, VII.*
89. Those rulers of the earth, who desirous of defeating each other, exert their utmost strength in battle without ever averting their faces, ascend after death directly to heaven.	44. The same.
90. No one should strike in a combat his enemy with concealed weapons, *nor with barbed arrows, nor with poisoned arrows, nor with darts kindled by fire.*	45. No one should strike in a combat his enemy with concealed weapons, *nor with poisoned arrows, nor with machines kindled by fire* (guns), *nor also with various stratagems.*
91. *Nor should he kill a person who is alighted on the ground,* nor one who is emasculated, nor one who has joined his hands as a supplicant, nor one who sits with dishevelled hair, nor one who says "I am thine."	46. *Nor should he kill a person who has climbed on a tree,* nor one who is emasculated, nor one who has joined his hands as a supplicant, nor one who sits with dishevelled hair, nor one who says "I am thine."

[131] *See* Manu, VII, 90, 91.

90. Na kūṭairāyudhairhanyāt yudhyamāno raṇe ripūn, *na karṇibhir nāpi digdhair nāgnijvalitatejanaiḥ.*

91. *Na ca hanyāt sthalārūḍham* na klībam na kṛtāñjalim, na muktakeśam nāsīnam na tavāsmīti vādinam.

Nītiprakāśikā, VII. 45, 46.

45. Na kūṭairāyudhairhanyāt yudhyamāno raṇe ripūn, *digdhair-agnyujjvalairyantraistantraiścaiva pṛthagvidhaiḥ.*

46. *Na hanyāt vṛksam ārūḍham* na klībam na kṛtāñjalim, na muktakeśam nāsīnam na tavāsmīti vādinam.

The punishment of any one who contravenes these laws was that he should inherit all the sins of him whom he thus kills unlawfully, and his victim would become heir to all the virtues of his murderer.[132] If what is most probable the Śukranīti and Nītiprakāśikā are of about the same age as our recension of the Mānavadharmaśāstra, the question as to firearms being known at that period can only be answered in the affirmative.

It appears that before the codification of the law in law-books, the rules and precepts regulating certain subjects seem to have been generally known among the people and even assumed already the form of verse. Otherwise it can hardly be explained that the very same ślokas are found in different authors, unless one is prepared to state that one must have copied them from another. But for such a supposition there exists no proof. It is rather more likely that they were common property and then embodied in the respective codes. There is not the slightest doubt that the interdict of the Mānavadharmaśāstra interfered a great deal with the popularity of firearms, and that though they continued to be used, they were less frequently or perhaps less openly employed. The Mahābhārata too contains many precepts by which mean, deceitful, and cruel behaviour is forbidden in war, but in reality those laws were often broken. The behaviour of the Kauravas against the Pāṇḍavas, whom they tried to burn

---

[132] As the Nītiprakāśikā differs somehow from the Mānavadharmaśāstra and from the Śukranīti we give here the following verses.

VII. 47. Na prasuptam na praṇatam na nagnam na nirāyudham
na yudhyamānam paśyantam na pareṇa samāgatam.
48. Āyudhavyasanam prāptam nārtam nātiparīkṣatam
na hīnam na parāvṛttam na ca valmīkam āśritam.
49. Na mukhe tṛṇinam hanyāt na striyo veṣadhāriṇam
etādṛśān bhaṭairvāpi ghātayan kilbiṣī bhavet.
50. Hanyamānasya yat kiñcit duṣkṛtam pūrvasañjitam
tat saṅgṛhya svasukṛtam tebhyo dadyāt tathāvidhaḥ.

With *na mukhe tṛṇinam hanyāt* (śl. 49) compare Mahābhārata, Rājadharma, XCVIII, 48a : Tṛṇapūrṇamukhaścaiva tavāsmīti ca yo vacet.

and to destroy by every imaginable means, the murder of the sleeping young Pāṇḍavas perpetrated by the Brahman Aśvatthāma; these and many more similar acts prove that though the laws of humanity were acknowledged *in abstracto* they were not as in the present day followed *in concreto*.

Besides the interference of these moral rules with the extension of the use of such weapons, another and perhaps even more potent reason can be produced. Firearms were such powerful engines of war, that every one, who possessed them, kept their construction and handling as secret as possible. This is, in fact, the real reason, why so few books treat on this subject, and why such works are so jealously kept secret that it is most difficult to get hold of them.

The Mahābhārata and Rāmāyaṇa are full of the description of wonderful divine firearms, the Āgneyāstra. It may be that a solid substratum of fact underlies these descriptions, but they are so adorned with wonders that they outrun all reality. Perhaps the reason of these exaggerations was to conceal the real element of truth underlying them.

Aurva, the son of the sage Ūrva, or, according to the Mahābhārata, a son of Cyavana, was scarcely born when he threatened to burn the world by the flame proceeding from him. This flame was then removed into the sea, where it is known as the submarine fire (baḍavāgni).[133] Aurva became later the guardian of the orphaned Sagara, whom he instructed in the Vedas and to whom he gave the fire weapon (āgneyāstra), by means of which Sagara regained the kingdom which his father Bāhu had lost. Agniveśa, the son of Agni, received, according to the Mahābhārata, the Āgneyāstra from Bharadvāja, and Agniveśa handed this weapon down to the son of Bharadvāja, Droṇa. This wonderful fire weapon plays an important part in the epic and dramatic literature, but it should not be overlooked that similar

[133] *See* Harivaṁśa, XIV.

wonderful weapons were ascribed also to other gods besides, *e.g.*, to Brahma, to Vāyu, to Varuṇa, &c., &c.[134]

Considering that Śukra or Uśanas is a member of the Bhārgava family, it seems a striking coincidence that the āgneyāstra is through Aurva also connected with the same family.

It may look strange that while gunpowder and firearms appear to have been known in India since immemorial times, and though we know that fireworks and firearms were always in use—the Portuguese, the first Europeans who came to this country, were struck at their landing with the display of both[135]—so few actual traces of them should be found in this country. But while admitting to a certain extent the truth of this observation, we must also consider that only very few old buildings have been preserved in India from ancient times, that we have nothing which can vie in age with Grecian antiquities, omitting Egyptian and Assyrian antiquities altogether. Yet still we can prove the existence of firearms by carved images of them being preserved in some ancient stone temples.

1. In the Madura District lies not far north from Rāmnāḍ (*Rāmanāthapura*) on the sea the ancient *Tirupallāṇi*. It is

---

134 *See* Harivaṁśa, XIV, 33.

Āgneyam astram labdhvā ca Bhargavāt Sagaro nṛpaḥ
jigāya pṛthivīm hatvā Tālajaṅghān sahaihayān.

Compare Mahābhārata, Ādiparva, CXXX, 39, 40.

39. Agniveśam mahābhāgam Bharadvājaḥ pratāpavān
pratyapādayat āgneyam astram astravidām varaḥ.

40. Agnestu jātassa munistato Bharatasattama
Bhāradvājam tad āgneyam mahāstram pratyapādayat.

See Śākuntala, III, 56, and Uttara Rāma Caritra, VI.

135 Castanheda says in his description of Vasco da Gama's entrance into Calicut: "The procession again set out, preceded by many trumpets and sacbuts sounding all the way; and one of the Nayres carried a caliver, which he fired off at intervals." *See* Elliot's History of India, VI, 467; compare Kerr's Collection of Voyages, Vol II, 364. According to Sir A. Phayre, the king of Pegu, when advancing in 1404 up the Irāvadi against the king Meng Khoung could neither land at nor attack Prome, as it was defended with cannon and muskets; *see* Journal, Asiatic Soc. Bengal, 1869, XXXVIII, p. 40.

celebrated throughout India, on account of its famous temple dedicated to Ādijagannātha, for pilgrims visit it from Benāres and other places in the north. The erection of this shrine goes back to a far distant period. On the outside of an ancient stone maṇḍapa are seen the figures of some soldiers carrying in their hands small firearms. The dress of these sepoys is also peculiar, as the belts round their waists are provided with little bells. The soldiers have slippers on their feet and a peculiar cap on their heads.

2. In *Kumbhaghoṇa* (Combaconum) is a temple devoted to Śārṅgapāṇi, *i.e.*, to Viṣṇu bearing in his hands his bow Śārṅga. It is one of the most ancient, largest, and most celebrated shrines in the Tanjore District. The height of the pagoda amounts to about 180 feet, and the numbers of its stories to eleven. On the left side of the front gate of the fifth story from the top is a king sitting in a chariot drawn by horses surrounded by his troops. In front of the king stand two sepoys with small firearms in their hands which look like pistols. The lower part of the pagoda is of solid stone, the higher ones and also the story just described partly of brick and partly of stone, *i.e.*, the principal figures are all made of stone, but they are every ten years covered with a layer of chalk and bricks. The Śārṅgapāṇi pagoda is said to be about 500 years old. Its sanctity and beauty is praised by seven Ālvārs, so that as it has not been rebuilt since that time, it must have been in existence when the sages lived. Tirupati is glorified by nine and Śrīraṅgam by ten Ālvārs.

3. In *Kāñcīpuram* (Conjeveram) is a famous maṇḍapa, which, as it rests on a hundred columns, is called *Śatastambhamaṇḍapa*, or *Nūṭikālmaṇḍapa* in Tamil. It was erected by Lakṣmīkumā-ratātācārya also called Koṭikanyādānatātācārya, as he was very rich and generous, and was said to have given a wedding present of 50 rupees to a krore (or ten millions) of girls. Being a Tātācārya he belonged to one of the highest

74 priestly families of the Vaisṇavabrāhmans, as the Tātācāryas trace their descent to Nādhamuni. He was the author of a work on Vedānta philosophy, and had at his own cost erected gopurams at Kāñcīpuram, Tirupati, Śrīraṅgam, and Tirumāliraṁśolai. His eldest son was Tirumalatātācārya, who administered the Anaguṇḍi kingdom for a while after the death of Vēṅkaṭapatirāya. When the Muhammedans occupied Kāñcīpuram Tirumalatatācārya lost all his riches.

The maṇḍapa is a square ; 12 columns face the eastern and western sides, 8 columns face the northern and southern ; besides these 96 columns 4 stand apart. On the 4th column of the north side, when coming from the west, is cut in solid stone, as the principal ornament of the column, a combat between soldiers. A trooper sits on horseback and a foot soldier aims with his firearm at his enemy. The maṇḍapa was erected about 1624 (the year being *tallakṣmīdyeśakhābde*).

4. In the precincts of the Tanjore temple are carved in stone on stone pillars opposite the " *Svarga ekadaśī*-gate sepoys with small carbines in their hands.

5. *In Pērūr*, a few miles from Coimbatore, is a celebrated Śiva temple and near it is a fine shrine, known as the Sabhāmaṇḍapa. On the base of its broad stone pillars stands a soldier with a gun in his hands. The date of the erection cannot be ascertained with exactness, and even popular belief does not ascribe to this maṇḍapa more than a few hundred years. As is usual with buildings in the south of the Dekkan Tirumala Nayak is occasionally named as its builder.

All these buildings, which, as we have seen, contain representations of firearms, are, according to our notions of antiquity, not very ancient, as, the Tirupallāṇi temple excepted, none of them is over 500 years old, but in judging the age of the subjects exhibited in the carvings of Indian temples, we should never lose sight of the fact that new subjects are not introduced in the architectural designs of the principal figures in any Indian ecclesiastical building. No architect, no one who erects a sacred pagoda at his own cost, will dare to represent in the chief carving of a conspicuous part of a building, as a big stone column is no doubt, a subject which is new and with which his countrymen were not familiar in times of yore, or which are not mentioned in the Śilpaśāstra, or the works on arts. This is a custom which is well known to every learned Brahman, and which is observed even now. Occasionally one sees in temples and other buildings odd, nay, even very indecent groups; but these quaint figures, which are by the bye never central ones, fulfil a special object, namely, to catch the evil eye, and so to protect the structure from any mischievous consequences. Whenever a new private house is built, such a figure will be displayed somewhere in a conspicuous place, and is generally removed after it had been in its place for some time and thus fulfilled its object. I have been assured on good authority that the Marīcipaṭala, a very ancient work on architecture, contains a description of architectural designs relating to firearms, but though I have written for this work, I am afraid I shall get it too late to verify this statement.[136]

Under these circumstances I cannot agree with the statement contained in Fergusson's excellent "History of Indian and Eastern Architecture" (p. 370), that "the date of the porch at Peroor is ascertained within narrow limits by the figure of a sepoy loading a musket being carved on the base of one of its pillars, and his costume and the shape of his arm are exactly those we find in contemporary pictures of the wars of Aurungzebe, or the early Mahrattas, in the beginning of the 18th century." I do not deny that the Sabhāmāṇḍapa may be comparatively new, but the figure of the sepoy with a musket in his hand can in no way settle the age of the building. As to the remarks concerning the costume of the soldier, there is

---

136 *See* Lists of Sanskrit Manuscripts in Private Libraries of Southern India, No. 5,610, lately published by me.

nothing to prove that his dress belongs to any certain period, and considering that the Hindu, if conservative in any thing, is especially so in his food and his dress, there is much probability that the uniform of the sepoy has also not been altered much in subsequent times. Moreover it must not be overlooked that the dress, especially the head-dress or turban varies according to caste and locality.

This remark leads me to refute an assertion made with some authority by Mr. W. F. Sinclair in the *Indian Antiquary* of September 1878. It is in a critical notice on a few ślokas extracted, not quite correctly though, from the Śukranīti by Mr. Rām Dās Sen.[137] In verse 136 we read : " The breech at the vent carries stone and powder and has a machinery which produces fire when striking." Alluding to this śloka Mr. Sinclair says : " From the evidence above given, it seems to me that if they (those verses) are not such interpolations the whole work must be a forgery of, at best, the 17th century, a period which I am led to select by the mention of the flint." Does Mr. Sinclair want to insinuate by this, that the Hindus did not know flints, nor their peculiar properties ? It is hardly credible that a nation, which is so observant, should have overlooked objects of such common occurrence ; or, if it knew them, that it should not have applied them to some use. Is it not perhaps judging others too much according to our own proficiencies, to intimate that, if Europeans did not apply flints or flintlocks to guns before the 17th century, no body else could have done so ? There is scarcely anything so common, so well known in this country, as the qualities of the flint ; in fact the Hindus are adepts in any thing connected with the art of making fire.

In the sixth book of the Nītiprakāśikā are enumerated all the articles which a king should take with him when setting out for a military expedition. After mentioning all sorts of provisions and arms mention is also made in the 51st śloka

[137] *Indian Antiquary*, 1878, p. 136.

of the following things: "and also the cotton of the silk-cotton tree and iron joined with flint."[138] This suggests at once the ordinary Indian tinderbox commonly called Rāma-svāmī, from the figure of the idol on its top.

The word for "*flint*" is in Tamil *śakkimukki* or *śakimuki*, and in Telugu *cakimuki*. If these terms are not onomato-poëtic, imitating the sound when the flint is struck, they may be regarded as derivations (*tadbhavams*) from the Sanskrit *śikhāmukha*, flame-mouth.

I trust thus to have proved that gunpowder and firearms were known in India in the most ancient times, that the statement in the Śukranīti about powder is supported by the Nītiprakāśikā of Vaiśampāyana, and that the quotation from the Rājalakṣmīnārāyaṇahṛdaya, a part of the ancient Atharvaṇarahasya, is an additional proof of it. I contend further that the knowledge of making gunpowder was never forgotten in India; but, that it was not earlier known in Europe is partly due to the isolated position of India, and partly also to the want of saltpetre in Europe, which prevented European nations from discovering the oxydizing properties of saltpetre. Moreover it must not be forgotten, that the preparation of gunpowder, even after it had become known, was kept everywhere a deep secret. The ancient Hindus enjoyed a well-deserved reputation as skilful artificers in iron and steel, the manipulation of which metals requires a considerable amount of ability, and these circumstances go surely far enough to justify the conclusion that the ancient Hindus were as well able to prepare firearms as the modern Hindus are now-a-days.[138] I further believe to have proved through quotations from the Nītiprakāśikā, the Naiṣadha, and even by incidental evidence from Manu that firearms were well known in ancient times, though the

[138] *See* Nītiprakāśikā, VI, 51; Śālmalītūlikām caiva vāpyaśmasārāśmasaṁyutām.—The *Rumpa* hillmen, *e.g.*, dig and smelt the iron-ore and cast it into musket-barrels.

interdict placed on them by Manu may have interfered somehow with their being generally used. On the other hand it must not be forgotten, that, though firearms existed, their construction was still in its infancy and that their application was very limited and did not diminish much the use of other arms. It ought also not to be overlooked that, as now, so also in ancient times, every thing connected with firearms and their improvement was surrounded with great mystery and the few books written on this subject were guarded like treasures and not communicated to the common crowd. The danger in handling firearms may also have deterred people from availing themselves of them so much as they otherwise would have done. Nevertheless the existence of guns and cannons in India in the earliest times seems to me to be satisfactorily proved from evidence supplied by some of the oldest Indian writings.

CHAPTER V.

ON THE ARMY ORGANISATION AND POLITICAL MAXIMS OF THE ANCIENT HINDUS.

THE SEVENTH SECTION OF THE FOURTH BOOK OF THE ŚUKRANĪTI.

1. Senā śastrāstrasaṁyuktamanuṣyādigaṇātmikā.
2. Svagamānyagamā ceti dvidhā, saiva pṛthak tridhā, daivyāsurī mānavī ca, pūrvapūrvābalādhikā;

---

1. An army is a numerous body consisting especially of men provided with weapons and missiles. Army.
2. It is of two kinds either self-moving or not self-moving; it is besides in a threefold manner an army either of gods, of demons or of human beings, each preceding being stronger than the succeeding.

3. Svagamā yā svayaṃgantrī, yānagā'nyagamā smṛtā ;
pādātam svagamam, cānyadrathāśvagajagam tridhā.
4. Sainyāt vinā naiva rājyam, na dhanam, na parākramaḥ.
5. Balino vaśagāḥ sarve durbalasya ca śatravaḥ
bhavantyalpajanasyāpi, nṛpasya tu na kim punaḥ.
6. Śārīram hi balam, śauryabalam, sainyabalam tathā
caturtham āstrikabalam, pañcamam dhībalam smṛtam,
ṣaṣṭam āyurbalam, tvetairupeto Viṣṇureva saḥ.
7. Na balena vinātyalpam ripum jetum kṣamāḥ sadā
devāsuranarāstvanyopāyairnityam bhavanti hi.
8. Balam eva ripornityam parājayakaram param
tasmāt balam abhedyam tu dhārayet yatnato nṛpaḥ.
9. Senābalam tu dvividham, svīyam maitram ca tad dvidhā,
maulasādyaskabhedābhyām, sārāsāram punardvidhā.

---

3. It is called self-moving, if it moves itself; not self-moving if it moves on vehicles. Infantry is self-moving; the not self-moving army moves in three ways, on carriages, horses and elephants.

4. If there is no army, there is no government, no wealth, no power.

5. All become the subjects even of a man of humble birth if he is strong, all his enemies if he is weak; is this not more so in the case of a king?

6. There surely exists physical strength, bravery, likewise military strength, the fourth is the strength of weapons, the fifth is called intellectual power, the sixth is vital power; who is endowed with these is indeed another Viṣṇu.

7. By force alone are gods, demons and men ever able to conquer even a very weak enemy.

8. An army is truly always the best means for the defeat of an enemy, a king should therefore zealously maintain an inconquerable army.

9. An armed force is of two kinds, it is either one's own, or it belongs to an ally; each with its own classes of

10. Aśikṣitam śikṣitam ca, gulmībhūtam agulmakam,
dattāstrādi svaśastrāstram, svavāhi dattavāhanam.
11. Saujanyāt sādhakam maitram, svīyam bhṛtyā prapālitam,
maulam bahvabdānubandhi, sādyaskam yattadanyathā.
12. Suyuddhakāmukam sāram, asāram viparītakam,
śikṣitam vyūhakuśalam, viparītam aśikṣitam.
13. Gulmībhūtam sādhikāri, svasvāmikam agulmakam,
dattāstrādi svāminā yat, svaśastrāstram ato'nyathā.
14. Kṛtagulmam svayaṃgulmam, tadvacca dattavāhanam
āraṇyakam Kirātādi yat svādhīnam svatejasā.
15. Utsṛṣṭam ripuṇā vāpi bhṛtyavarge niveśitam
bhedādhīnam kṛtam śatroḥ sainyam śatrubalam smṛtam,
ubhayam durbalam proktam, kevalam sādhakam na tat.

---

reserve and line, and these again are in a twofold manner divided into efficient and inefficient men.

10. It is either trained or not trained, formed or not formed into corps, provided or providing itself with arms, provided or providing itself with vehicles.

11. An allied army is useful when kindly treated, one's own is maintained by pay; the reserve is of many years' standing, the line differs in this respect.

12. The efficient is eager for a good fight, the inefficient is the reverse; the trained is clever in tactics, the untrained is the reverse.

13. The army formed in corps has a commander, that which is its own master is not well arranged in corps; the one has received arms from the king, the other which carries its own arms differs in this respect.

14. The forester corps, *i.e.*, the Kirātas and similar tribes, which is subdued by the power of the king, is formed into corps or has formed itself into corps, after having been supplied with vehicles.

15. The army of the enemy which was given up by the foe, or which having entered his service is won over by dissension, is still regarded as hostile; both are regarded as weak, and especially as not trustworthy.

16. Samairniyuddhakuśalairvyāyāmairnatibhistathā
vardhayet bāhuyuddārtham bhojyaiḥ śārīrakam balam.
17. Mṛgayābhistu vyāghrāṇām śastrāstrābhyāsataḥ sadā
vardhayet śūrasaṁyogāt saṁyak śauryabalam nṛpaḥ.
18. Senābalam subhṛtyā tu tapobhyāsaistathāstrikam
vardhayet śāstracaturasaṁyogāt dhībalam sadā.
19. Satkriyābhiścirasthāyi nityam rājyam bhavet yathā,
svagotre tu tathā kuryāt tat āyurbalam ucyate;
yāvat gotre rājyam asti tāvat eva sa jīvati.
20. Caturguṇam hi pādātam aśvato dhārayet sadā,
pañcamāṁśānstu vṛṣabhān aṣṭāṁśāñśca kramelakān;
21. Caturthāṁśān gajān uṣṭrāt, gajārdhāñśca rathānstathā
rathāt tu dviguṇam rājā bṛhannālikam eva ca.

---

16. One should increase the physical strength for pugilistic combats by diet and by athletic exercises and wrestling with equals and with those who are experts in close fighting.

17. A king should always well encourage bravery by tiger-hunts, by practice with weapons and arms and through association with brave men.

18. He should keep up his military strength by good pay, but the strength of his weapons by penance and practice; and his intellectual power by having always intercourse with wise persons.

19. That his kingdom may always be long lasting in his family, he should effect by good deeds, this is called vital power; as long as the kingdom remains in his family, he lives indeed.

Proportion of different arms to each other.

20. A king should always maintain four times as many foot-soldiers as horses, for every five horses one bull, for every eight horses one camel;

21. for every four camels one elephant, for every two elephants one chariot, for every chariot two big guns.[139]

---

139 *See* pp. 4–6. The proportion of the different parts to each other is represented by 5 chariots, 10 elephants, 40 camels, 64 bulls, 320 horses, and 1,280 men.

22. Padātibahulam sainyam madhyāśvam tu gajālpakam
tathā vṛṣoṣṭrasāmānyam rakṣet nāgādhikam na hi.

23. Savayassāraveṣauca śastrāstram tu pṛthak śatam
laghunālikayuktānām padātīnām śatatrayam ;

24. Aśītyaśvān ratham caikam bṛhannāladvayam tathā,
uṣṭrān daśa gajau dvau tu śakaṭau ṣoḍaśarṣabhān ;

25. Tathā lekhakaṣaṭkam hi mantritritayam eva ca,
dhārayet nṛpatiḥ samyak vatsare lakṣakarṣabhāk.[140]

---

22. He should keep an army with many foot-soldiers, with a moderate number of horses, but with few elephants; likewise with a small number of bulls and camels, but not with many elephants.

23. A prince, who gets a lac of karṣas a year, should maintain well with weapons and missiles respectively one hundred men, 300 foot-soldiers with small firearms, who are (all) equal in age, strength and dress ;

24. eighty horses and one chariot; likewise two big guns ; ten camels, two elephants, two waggons and sixteen bulls ;

25. likewise also six clerks and certainly three ministers.

---

[140] *See* Līlāvatī, śl. 2–4.

2. Varāṭakānām daśakadvayam yat sā kākiṇī tāśca paṇaścatasraḥ
te ṣoḍaśa dramma ihāvagamyo drammaistathā ṣoḍaśabhiśca niṣkaḥ.

3. Tulyā yavābhyām kathitātra guñjā vallaistriguñjo dharaṇam ca te'ṣṭau
gadyāṇakastaddvayam indratulyairvallaistathaiko dhaṭakaḥ pradiṣṭaḥ.

4. Dasārdhaguñjam pravadanti māṣam māṣāhvayaiṣṣoḍaśabhiśca karṣaḥ
karṣaiścaturbhiśca palam tulā tacchatam suvarṇasya suvarṇasañjñam.

That is 20 *Varāṭakas* are 1 Kākiṇī, 4 *Kākiṇīs* 1 Paṇa, 16 *Paṇas* 1 Dramma, 16 *Drammas* 1 Niṣka. 2 *Yavas* are 1 Guñja, 3 *Guñjas* 1 Valla, 8 *Vallas* 1 Dharaṇa, 2 *Dharaṇas* 1 Gadyāṇaka and 14 Vallas 1 Dhaṭaka. Further 10½ *Guñjas* are 1 *Māṣa*, 16 Māṣas 1 *Karṣa*, 4 Karṣas 1 *Pala*, 100 Palas 1 *Tulā* and a Tulā is equal to a *Suvarṇa*.

26. Sambhāradānabhogārthaṃ dhanam sārdhasahasrakam,
lekhakārthe śatam māsi mantryarthe tu śatatrayam ;
27. Triśatam dāraputrārthe vidvadarthe śatadvayam
sādyaśvapadagārtham hi rājā catussahasrakam ;
28. Gajoṣṭravṛṣanālārtham vyayīkuryāt catuśśatam
śeṣam kośe dhanam sthāpyam rājñā sārddhasahasrakam.
29. Prativarṣam svaveśārtham sainikebhyo dhanam haret.

Expenditure.

26. The king should spend on provisions, largesse and pleasure fifteen hundred karṣas, on clerks one hundred a month, but on ministers three hundred ;

27. on his wife and son three hundred, on learned men two hundred, on elephant-drivers, horses (cavalry) and foot-soldiers four thousand ;

28. on the straw for elephants, camels and bulls four hundred. The remaining money fifteen hundred karṣas should be deposited by the king in the treasury.[141]

29. The king should deduct every year a sum of money from the soldiers for their dress.

---

[141] The 100,000 Karṣas will be expended as follows :—

	Per Mensem.	
Provisions, largesse and pleasure	1,500	Karṣas.
Clerks (one clerk at 16$\frac{2}{3}$ K.)	100	,,
Ministers (one minister at 100 K.)	300	,,
Wife and family	300	,,
Learned men	200	,,
Elephant drivers, cavalry and infantry	4,000	,,
Straw	400	,,
Reserve funds	1,500	,,
Total ..	8,300	..,,

or 99,600 Karṣas, *i.e.*, about a lac of Karṣas a year.

The title of a sovereign depends on the yearly income his country yields to him. A *Sāmanta* is called a prince who receives up to 3 lacs, a *Māṇḍalika* gets up to 10 lacs, a *Rāja* up to 20 lacs, a *Mahārāja* up to 50 lacs, a *Svarāṭ* up to a krore or ten millions, a *Saṁrāṭ* up to 10 krores, and a *Virāṭ* up to 25 krores. To a *Sārvabhauma* is subjected the whole earth with its seven islands.

30. Lohasāramayaḥ·cakrasugamo, mañcakāsanaḥ,
svāndolāyitarūḍhastu, madhyamāsanasārathiḥ,
31. Śastrāstrasandhāryudara, iṣṭacchāyo, manoramaḥ,
evaṁvidho ratho rājñā rakṣyo nityam sadaśvakaḥ.
32. Nīlatālurnīlajihvo vakradanto hyadantakaḥ
dīrghadveṣī krūramadaḥ tathā pṛṣṭhavidhūnakaḥ.
33. Daśāṣṭonanakho mando bhūviśodhanapucchakaḥ
evaṁvidho' niṣṭagajo, viparītaḥ śubhāvahaḥ.
34. Bhadro, mandro, mṛgo, miśro gajo jātyā caturvidhaḥ.

---

30. An iron-made carriage, well going on wheels, provided with a couch as a seat; on which is fixed a swing, with a charioteer on the middle seat; Carriage.

31. with an interior carrying weapons and missiles, giving agreeable shade, and (altogether) beautiful—such a carriage provided with good horses, should always be kept by the king.

32. An elephant with a dark blue palate, a dark blue tongue, a crooked tooth, toothless, which bears malice a long time, has fierce rut, waddles likewise with his hinder part; Elephant.

33. with ten or seven claws, is slow, which rubs the ground with his tail—such an elephant is undesirable, the opposite confers benefits.

34. The elephant is of four kinds according to its race; either a Bhadra (*propitious*), Mandra (*pleasing*), Mṛga (*deer*), or a Miśra (mixed).

See Śukranīti, I, 184–187.

184. Sāmantaḥ sa nṛpaḥ prokto yāvat lakṣatrayāvadhi
tadūrdhvam daśalakṣānto nṛpo māṇḍalikaḥ smṛtaḥ.
185. Tadūrdhvam tu bhavet rājā yāvat viṁśatilakṣakaḥ.
pañcāśat lakṣaparyanto mahārājaḥ prakīrtitaḥ
186. Tatastu koṭiparyantaḥ svarāṭ, saṁrāṭ tataḥ param
daśakoṭimito yāvat, virāṭ tu tadanantaram
187. Pañcāśat koṭiparyantaḥ, sārvabhaumastataḥ param
saptadvīpā ca pṛthivī yasya vaśyā bhavet sadā.

35. Madhvābhadantaḥ sabalaḥ samāngo vartulākṛtiḥ
sumukho' vayavaśreṣṭho jñeyo bhadra gajaḥ sadā.

36. Sthūlakukṣī siṁhadṛk ca bṛhattvāggalaśuṇḍakaḥ
madyamāvayavo dhīrghakāyo mandragajassmṛtaḥ.

37. Tanukaṇṭhadantakarṇaśuṇḍaḥ sthūlāksa eva hi
suhrasvādharameḍhrastu vāmano mṛgasañjñakaḥ.

38. Eṣām lakṣmairvimilito gajo miśra iti smṛtaḥ;
bhinnam bhinnam pramāṇam tu trayāṇām api kīrtitam.

39. Gajamāne hyaṅgulam syāt aṣṭabhistu yavodaraiḥ
caturviṁśatyaṅgulaistaiḥ karaḥ prokto manīṣibhiḥ;

40. Saptahastonnatirbhadre hyaṣṭahastapradīrghatā
pariṇāho daśakaraḥ udarasya bhavet sadā.

---

35. The elephant which has honey-coloured teeth, is strong, well proportioned, has a globular shape, good head and excellent limbs, is always known as a Bhadra.

36. The elephant which has a huge belly, and a lion's eye, a thick skin, throat and trunk, middle-sized limbs, a long body, is styled Mandra.

37. The elephant which has a small neck, teeth, ears and trunk, a peculiarly big eye, but a very small underlip and membrum, and is dwarfish, is called Mṛga.

38. The elephant which is mixed with the marks of these three, is called Miśra. It is also mentioned, that these three elephants differ respectively in size.

39. An aṅgula (the breadth of a thumb), when applied for the measurement of an elephant, should consist exactly of eight corns, 24 such aṅgulas are declared by wise men to be an elephantine hand.

40. The height of a Bhadra is 7 cubits, its length 8 cubits, the circumference of its belly should always be 10 cubits.

41. Pramāṇam mandramṛgayorhastahīnam kramāt ataḥ
kathitam dairghyasāmyam tu munibhirbhadramandrayoḥ.

42. Bṛhadbhrūgaṇḍaphālastu dhṛtaśīrṣagatiḥ sadā
gajaḥ śreṣṭhastu sarveṣām śubhalakṣaṇasaṁyutaḥ.

43. Pañcayavāṅgulenaiva vājimānam pṛthak smṛtam,
catvāriṁśāṅgulamukho vājī yaścottamottamaḥ.

44. Ṣaṭtriṁśadaṅgulamukho hyuttamaḥ parikīrtitaḥ
dvātriṁśadaṅgulamukho madhyamaḥ sa udāhṛtaḥ.

45. Aṣṭāviṁśatyaṅgulo yo mukhe nīcaḥ prakīrtitaḥ ;
vājinām mukhamanēna sarvāvayavakalpanā.

46. Auccam tu mukhamānena triguṇam parikīrtitam.

---

41. The size of a Mandra and Mṛga is respectively one cubit less ; though the length of a Mandra and Mṛga is by sages declared to be the same.

42. The best of all elephants is surely that, which has large brows, cheek and forehead, bears always its head firmly, and is endowed with auspicious marks.

43. By an aṅgula of only five barley grains is the equine Horse. measure separately recorded. A horse whose head is 40 aṅgulas (long) is regarded as the very best.

44. A horse whose head is 36 aṅgulas long is surely considered a very fair one ; a horse whose head is 32 aṅgulas long is declared to be a middling one.

45. A horse whose head is 28 aṅgulas long is regarded as an inferior one. The proportion of all the limbs of a horse is measured by the length of the head.

46. The height is declared to be three times the length of the head.

47. Śiromaṇim samārabhya pucchamūlāntam eva hi
tritīyāṁśādhikam dairghyam mukhamānāt caturguṇam
pariṇāhastūdarasya triguṇastryaṅgulādhikaḥ.
48. Śmaśruhīnamukhaḥ kāntapragalbhōttuṅganāsikaḥ
dīrghoddhatagrīvamukho hrasvakuksikhuraśrutiḥ;
49. Turapracaṇḍavegaśca haṁsameghasamasvanaḥ
nātikrūro nātimṛdurdevasatvo manoramaḥ;
sukāntigandhavarṇaśca sadgunabhramarānvitaḥ.
50. Bhramarastu dvidhāvarto vāmadakṣiṇabhedataḥ
pūrṇo'pūrṇaḥ punardvedhā dīrgho hrasvastathaiva ca.
51. Strīpundehe vāmadakṣau yathoktaphaladau kramāt
na tathā viparītau tu śubhāśubhaphalapradau.

---

47. The length beginning with the poll up to the very root of the tail is $1\frac{1}{3}$ of the height, or four times the length of the head, the circumference of the belly is three times the length of the head and three aṅgulas besides.

48. A horse which has a face without whiskers, is beautiful, courageous, has a high nose, a long and raised crest and head, a short belly, hoof and ear;

49. is impetuous and fast, neighs like a cloud or a goose (*haṁsa*), is neither too fierce nor too mild, is a pleasing *Devasatva* (godlike); it is of excellent beauty, flavour, and colour, and endowed with feathers of good qualities.

Feathers of the horse.

50. A feather is turned in two ways, either to the right or left, is full or not full, and is further in a two-fold manner either long or short.

51. The left-and right-side feathers of mares and stallions are respectively, as said, auspicious, but not thus, if they are on opposite sides; for they have then neither good nor bad consequences.

52. Nīcordhvatiryaṅmukhataḥ phalabhedo bhavet tayoḥ
śaṅkhacakragadāpadmavedisvastikasannibhaḥ;
53. Prāsādatoraṇadhanussupūrṇakalaśākṛtiḥ
svastikasraṅmīnakhaḍgaśrīvatsābhaḥ śubho bhramaḥ.
54. Nāsikāgre lalāṭe ca śaṅkhe kaṇṭheca mastake
āvarto jāyate yeṣām te dhanyāsturagottamāḥ.
55. Hṛdi skandhe gale caiva kaṭideśe tathaiva ca
nābhau kukṣau ca pārśvāgre madhyamāḥ samprakīrtitāḥ.
56. Lalāṭe yasya cāvartadvitayasya samudbhavaḥ
mastake ca tṛtīyasya pūrṇaharṣo'yam uttamaḥ.
57. Pṛṣṭhavaṁśe yadāvarto yasyaikaḥ samprajāyate
sakarotyaśvasaṅghātān svāminaḥ sūryasañjñakaḥ.
58. Trayo yasya lalāṭasthā āvartāstiryaguttarāḥ
trikūṭaḥ sa parijñeyo vājī vṛddhikaraḥ sadā.

---

52. There will be a difference in efficiency according as its mouth is low, high or oblique. If the feather is like a shell, wheel, club, lotus, altar, portico;

53. like an upper story, arch, bow, well-filled pitcher, like a triangle, chaplet, fish, sword, a mole on the breast, it is a lucky feather.

54. The horses on whose tip of the nose, forehead, temple, throat or skull exists a feather, are the best.

55. Those horses are regarded as middling, which have it on the heart, shoulder, neck, likewise on the hips, on the navel, belly and foreribs.

56. That horse is the best *Pūrṇaharṣa* (fulljoy) on whose temple rises a double feather, and on whose skull rises a third.

57. That horse on whose backbone rises one feather, is called *Sūrya* (sun) and procures to his master masses of horses.

58. That horse on whose forehead stand three oblique feathers, is called *Trikūṭa* (threepeaked) and it gives always prosperity to its master.

59. Evam eva prakāreṇa trayo grīvam samāśritāḥ
samāvartāḥ sa vājīśo jāyate nṛpamandire.
60. Kapolasthau yadāvartau dṛśyete yasya vājinaḥ
yaśovṛddhikarau proktau rājyavṛddhikarau matau.
61. Eko vātha kapolastho yasyāvartaḥ pradṛśyate
sarvanāmā sa vikhyātaḥ sa icchet svāmināśanam.
62. Gaṇḍasaṁstho yadāvarto vājino dakṣiṇāśritaḥ
sa karoti mahāsaukhyam svāminam śivasañjñikaḥ.
63. Sahṛidvāmāśritaḥ krūraḥ prakaroti dhanakṣayam
indrākṣau tāvubhau śastau nṛparājyavivṛddhidau.
64. Karṇamūle yadāvartau stanamadhye tathā parau
vijayākhyau ubhau tau tu yuddhakāle yaśaḥpradau.
65. Skandhapārśve yadāvartau sa bhavet padmalakṣaṇaḥ
karoti vividhān padmān svāminaḥ santatam sukham.

---

59. That is the best horse in the King's palace, on whose neck are also placed three feathers in such a manner.

60. The two feathers which on a horse's cheeks are seen standing, are called augmentors of fame and are esteemed as augmentors of kingship.

61. A horse, on whose left cheek is observed a feather standing, is called *Sarvanāmā*, and it may wish for the destruction of its master.

62. The horse on whose right cheek stands a feather renders his master very happy, it is called *Śiva* (prosperous).

63. That bad (feather) on the left side of the heart produces loss of wealth, the two excellent *Indrākṣa* (Indra's eyes) increase the kingdom of the king.

64. A horse which has two feathers on the root of the ear, or which has also two on the middle of the breast; these both are called *Vijaya* (victory) and give glory in time of war.

65. A horse, which has two feathers on the shoulderblade, should be called *Padma* (wealth), it gives many virtues and continual happiness to its master.

66. Nāsāmadhye yadāvarta eko vā yadi vā trayam
cakravartī sa vijñeyo vājī bhūpālasañjñikaḥ.
67. Kaṇṭhe yasya mahāvarta ekaḥ śreṣṭhaḥ prajāyate
cintāmaṇiḥ sa vijñeyaḥ cintitārthasukhapradaḥ.
68. Śuklākhyau phālakaṇṭhasthau āvartau vṛddikīrtidau.
69. Yasyāvartau vakragatau kukṣyante vājino yadi,
sa nūnam mṛtyum āpnoti kuryāt vā svāmināśanam.
70. Jānusaṁsthā yadāvartāḥ pravāsakleśakārakāḥ,
vājimeḍhre yadāvarto vijayaśrīvināśanaḥ.
71. Trikasaṁstho yadāvartaḥ trivargasya praṇāśanaḥ
pucchamūle yadāvarto dhūmaketuranarthakṛt,
guhyapucchatrikāvartī sa kṛtāntabhayapradaḥ.

---

66. According as there is one feather or there are three feathers on the midst of the nose, the horse is called *Cakravartī* or *Bhūpāla.*

67. The horse on whose throat is one very good large feather, is called *Cintāmaṇi,* bestowing every imaginary happiness and wealth.

68. Two feathers, which stand on the forehead and throat (and are) called *Śukla* (bright), give fame and prosperity.

69. If at the extremity of the belly of a horse are two curved feathers, that will surely incur death or cause the destruction of its master.

70. If there are feathers on the knees, they cause troubles and sojournings ; if a feather is on the penis of a horse, it ruins victory and prosperity.

71. If a feather stands on the lower spine it is the destroyer of three things,[142] if the feather *Dhūmaketu* (comet) is on the root of the tail, it produces trouble ; a horse which has a feather on the anus, tail and lower spine causes fear of death.

---

[142] Dharma, artha, kāma.

72. Madhyadaṇḍā pārśvagamā saiva śatapadī kace
atiduṣṭāṅguṣṭhamitā dīrghāduṣṭā yathā yathā.

73. Aśrupātahanugaṇḍahṛdgalaprōthavastiṣu
katiśaṅkhajānumuṣkakakunnābhigudeṣu ca ;
dakṣakukṣau dakṣapāde tvaśubho bhramaraḥ sadā.

74. Galamadhye pṛṣṭhamadhye uttaroṣṭhe' dhare tathā,
karṇanetrāntare vāmakukṣau caiva tu pārśvayōḥ
ūruṣu ca śubhāvarto vājinām agrapādayoḥ.

75. Āvartau sāntarau phāle sūryacandrau śubhapradau
militau tau madhyaphalau hyatilagnau tu duṣphalau.

76. Āvartatritayam phāle śubham cordhvam tu sāntaram
aśubham cātisaṁlagnam āvartadvitayam tathā.

---

72. If the feather is in the midst formed like a stick, is turned towards the sides, is on the head, it is a *Śatapadī*; it is very bad if it is a thumb broad, in proportion as it is long it is good.

73. If a feather is on the place where the tears fall, on the cheek, jaw, heart, neck and abdomen, on the buttock, temple, knee, penis, hump, navel and anus, if on the right belly, on the right foot, that is always an unlucky feather.

74. A good horse-feather is on the middle of the neck, on the middle of the back, on the upperlip, likewise on the underlip, between eye and ear, on the left belly, on the two sides, on the loins and on the frontlegs.

75. Two feathers apart on the forehead, *Sūryacandrau* (sun and moon) give luck, if not apart they are pretty good, but surely unlucky, if much mixed.

76. Three perpendicular and apart standing feathers on the forehead are lucky, but two (similar) much mixed feathers are unlucky.

77. Trikoṇatritayam phāle āvartānām tu duḥkhadam
galamadhye śubhaḥ tvekaḥ sarvāśubhanivāraṇaḥ.

78. Adhomukhaḥ śubhaḥ pāde phāle cordhvamukho bhramaḥ
nacaivātyaśubhā pṛṣṭhamukhī śatapadī matā.

79. Mēḍhrasya paścāt bhramarī stanī vājī sa cāśubhaḥ,
bhramaḥ karṇasamīpe tu śṛṅgī caikaḥ sa ninditaḥ.

80. Grīvōrdhvapārśve bhramarī hyekaraśmiḥ sa caikataḥ
pādordhvamukhabhramarī kilōtpāṭī sa ninditaḥ.

81. Śubhāśubhau bhramau yasmin sa vājī madhyamaḥ smṛtaḥ
mukhe patsu sitaḥ pañcakalyāṇośvaḥ sadā mataḥ.

---

77. Three triangular feathers on the forehead are unlucky; but one lucky feather on the middle of the neck, suspends all bad ones.

78. A feather on the foot with its face downwards, and one on the forehead with its face upwards, is lucky, but the *Śatapadī* is not regarded as very lucky, if it is turned towards the back.

79. If the feather is a *Stanī* (having a nipple) behind the penis, the horse is also unlucky, but if the feather is a *Śṛṅgī* (horned) near the ear, it is blamed.

80. The feather *Ekaraśmi* (having one string) on one side on the upper part of the neck, (and) the feather *Kīlotpāṭī* (*destroying bolts*) on the foot with its face upwards is despised.

81. The horse in which are lucky and unlucky feathers is a *Madhyama* (middling), that which is white on the head and feet is always esteemed as a *Pañcakalyāṇa* (excellent for five things).

82. Sa eva hṛdaye skandhe pucche śveto'ṣṭamaṅgalaḥ,
karṇe śyāmaḥ śyāmakarṇaḥ sarvataḥ tvekavarṇabhāk.
83. Tatrāpi sarvataḥ śveto medhyaḥ pūjyaḥ sadaiva hi,
vaiḍūryasannibhe netre yasya sto jayamaṅgalaḥ.
84. Miśravarṇaḥ tvekavarṇaḥ pūjyaḥ syāt sundaro yadi.
85. Kṛṣṇapādo hayo nindyaḥ tathā śvetaikapādapi
rūkṣo dhūsaravarṇaśca gardhabhābho'pi ninditaḥ.
86. Kṛṣṇatāluḥ kṛṣṇajihvaḥ kṛṣṇoṣṭhaśca vininditaḥ
sarvataḥ kṛṣṇavarṇo yaḥ pucche śvetaḥ sa ninditaḥ.
87. Suśvetaphālatilako viddho varṇāntareṇa ca
sa vājī dalabhañjī tu yasya so'pyatininditaḥ.

---

82. The horse which is white on the heart, shoulder and tail is an *Aṣṭamaṅgala* (excellent for eight things), that, which has a black ear and only one other color (besides) is a *Śyāmakarṇa* (black ear).

83. That which except there (the black ear) is totally white, is always to be worshipped as a *Medhya* (sacrificial), that whose eyes are like a turquoise is a *Jayamaṅgala* (excellent for victory).

84. Whether a horse has different colours or has one colour it should always be esteemed, if it is beautiful.

85. A horse with a black foot is despisable, likewise if it has only one white foot, one which is rough and is grey-coloured is always blamed as looking like a donkey.

86. A horse with a black palate, black tongue and black lip is despised; a horse which is everywhere black but is white at the tail is blamed.

87. That horse which has on its forehead a very white mark, which is perforated by another colour is a *Dalabhañjī* (Piece breaking) and its owner is also much blamed.

88. Saṁhanyāt varṇajān doṣān snigdhavarṇo bhavet yadi;
balādhikaśca sugatirmahān sarvāṅgasundaraḥ,
nātikrūraḥ sadā pūjyo bhramādyairapi dūṣitaḥ.
89. Pariṇāho vṛṣamukhāt udare tu caturguṇaḥ
sa kakut triguṇoccam tu sārdhatriguṇadīrghatā.
90. Saptatālo vṛṣaḥ pūjyo guṇairetairyuto yadi
na sthāyī na ca vai mandaḥ suvoḍhā hyaṅgasundaraḥ,
nātikrūraḥ supṛṣṭhaḥ ca vṛṣabhaḥ śreṣṭha ucyate.
91. Triṁśadyojanagantā vā pratyaham bhāravāhakaḥ
daśatālaśca[143] sudṛḍhaḥ sumukhoṣṭraḥ praśasyate.
92. Śatam āyurmanuṣyāṇām gajānām paramam smṛtam
manuṣyagajayorbālyam yāvat viṁśativatsaram.

---

88. If however the colour is agreeable it suspends all faults arising from colour; and a horse which is very strong, goes well, is large, beautiful in all its limbs, not very fierce is always to be honoured, even if spoiled by feathers.

Bull.

89. The circumference of the belly is four times the size of a bull's head, three times its size is the height and three and a half times its length.

90. A bull which is seven spans high, if provided with good qualities, is to be respected. A bull which does neither stop, nor is slow, carries well, is moreover beautiful in limbs, is not very fierce, has a good back; is called the best bull.

Camel.

91. A camel, which goes daily thirty yojanas while carrying loads, is ten spans high, very strong and has a fine head, is praised.

Age of men and elephants.

92. A hundred years is recorded as the longest life of men and elephants, the youth of men and elephants is reckoned up to twenty years.

---

143 "navatālaśca" is a different reading in one MS.

93. Nṛṇām hi madhyamam yāvat ṣaṣṭivarṣam vayassmṛtam
aśītivatsaram yāvat gajasya madhyamam vayaḥ.
94. Catustriṁśat tu varṣāṇām aśvasyāyuḥ param smṛtam
pañcaviṁśati varṣam hi param āyurvṛṣoṣṭrayoḥ.
95. Bālyam aśvavṛṣoṣṭrāṇām pañcasaṁvatsaram matam
madhyamam yāvat ṣōḍaśābdam vārdhakyam tu tataḥ param.
96. Dantānām udgamairvarṇairāyurjñeyam vṛṣāśvayoḥ
aśvasya ṣaṭ sitā dantāḥ prathamābde bhavanti hi.
97. Kṛṣṇalohitavarṇāstu dvitīye'bde hyadhogatāḥ,
tṛtīye'bde tu sandaṁśau madhyamau patitodgatau.
98. Tatpārśvavartinau tau tu caturthe punarudgatau,
antyau dvau pañcamābde tu sandaṁśau punarudgatau.

---

93. The middle age of men is estimated to last up to sixty years, the middle age of an elephant up to eighty years.

Age of horses.

94. On the other hand thirty-four years are considered as the utmost age of horses, while twenty-five years are surely the highest age of bulls and camels.

Age of bulls and camels.

95. The youth of horses, bulls and camels extends up to five years, the middle age up to sixteen years, but afterwards is old age.

Teeth of horses.

96. By the growth and colour of the teeth the age of bulls and horses can be known. Six white teeth are surely in the first year of a horse,

97. but in the second year the lower teeth become dark red coloured, in the third year the middle biters fall out and come again ;

98. in the fourth year those two on their sides fall out and come again, in the fifth year the two biters at the end fall out and come again ;

99. Madhyapārśvāntagau dvau dvau kramāt kṛṣṇau ṣaḍ-abdataḥ;
navamābdāt kramāt pītau tau sitau dvādaśābdataḥ.
100. Daśapañcābdataḥ tau tu kācābhau kramataḥ smṛtau
aṣṭādaśābdataḥ tau hi madhvābhau bhavatah kramāt.
101. Śaṅkhābhau caikaviṁśābdāt caturviṁśābdataḥ sadā
chidram sañcalanam pāto dantānām ca trike trike.
102. Prothe suvalayastisraḥ pūrṇāyuryasya vājinaḥ,
yathā yathā tu hīnāstā hīnam āyustathā tathā.
103. Jānūtpāto tvoṣṭhavādyo dhūtapṛṣṭho jalāsanaḥ
gatimadhyāsanaḥ pṛṣṭhapātī paścādgamordhvapāt.
104. Sarpajihvo rūkṣakāntirbhīruraśvo'tininditaḥ,
sacchidraphālatilako nindya āśrayakṛt tathā.

---

99. from the sixth year the two middle, side and end teeth become gradually black, each pair becomes in its turn yellow from the ninth year; and white from the twelfth year.

100. From the fifteenth year each pair is said to become in its turn glass-coloured, from the eighteenth each pair becomes by degrees honey-coloured;

101. from the twenty-first year each pair becomes shell-coloured, from the twenty-fourth each pair becomes in each third year hollow (24th–26th year), shaky (27th–29th), and falls out (30th–32nd).

102. The horse which has three deep wrinkles in the nostrils has a long life; in proportion as the wrinkles are deficient the life is also limited.

103. A horse which jumps up on its knees, makes a noise with its lips; sits down in water, stands still in the midst of the road, falls on its back, jumps upwards while going backwards,

104. which has a tongue like a serpent, is of disagreeable colour, and timid is much despised; despised is also a horse whose mark on the forehead has flaws and which stands often still.

105. Vṛṣasyāṣṭau sitā dantāḥ caturthe'bde'khilāḥ smṛtāḥ,
dvāvantyau patitotpannau pañcame'bde hi tasya vai.
106. Ṣaṣṭhe tūpāntyau bhavataḥ saptame tatsamīpagau,
aṣṭame patitotpannau madhyamau daśanau khalu.
107. Kṛṣṇapītasitaraktaśaṅkhacchāyau dvike dvike
kramāt hi dve ca bhavataḥ calanam patanam tataḥ.
108. Uṣṭrasyoktaprakāreṇa vayojñānam tu vā bhavet.
109. Prerakākarṣakamukho'ṅkuśo gajavinigrahe
hastipakairgajastena vineyassugamāya hi.
110. Khalīnasyordhvakhaṇḍau dvau pārśvagau dvādaśāṅgu-lau
tatpārśvāntargatābhyām tu sudṛḍhābhyām tathaiva ca.

---

105. Eight complete white teeth are mentioned as existing in the fourth year of the bull, in its fifth year two molars fall out and rise again ; *Teeth of a bull.*

106. in the sixth year the two next to the molars, in the seventh the two next ones, in the eighth year the two middle biters fall and come again.

107. Every second year they get by degrees black, yellow, white, red and shell-coloured. Each pair becomes gradually loose and falls out.[144]

108. The knowledge of the age of a camel may be likewise reckoned according to the above-mentioned rule. *Age of a camel.*

109. For training an elephant a hook is used by the elephant-drivers, which has one point for driving on and another for drawing back ; by this hook the elephant is guided to go well. *Elephant-training.*

110. The two upwards and sideways pointing parts of a bridle-bit are respectively on the whole twelve aṅgulas long, with two inside but very strong pieces, *Bridle.*

---

[144] Black in the 9th and 10th year, yellow in the 11th and 12th, white in the 13th and 14th, red in the 15th and 16th, shell-coloured in the 17th and 18th, in the 19th the end teeth get loose, in the 20th the end teeth fall out and the last but one become loose, &c. &c.

111. Vārakākarṣakhaṇḍābhyām rajvarthavalayair yutau
evaṁvidhakhalīnena vaśīkuryāt tu vājinam.
112. Nāsikākarṣarajvā tu vṛṣoṣṭram vinayet bhṛśam
tīkṣṇāgro yaḥ saptaphālaḥ syāt eṣām malaśodhane.
113. Sutāḍanairvineyā hi manuṣyāḥ paśavaḥ sadā,
sainikāstu viśeṣeṇa na te vai dhanadaṇḍataḥ.
114. Anūpe tu vṛṣāśvānām gajoṣṭrāṇām tu jāṅgale
sādhāraṇe padātīnām niveśāt rakṣaṇam bhavet.
115. Śatam śatam yojanānte sainyam rāṣṭre niyojayet.
116. Gajoṣṭravṛṣabhāśvāḥ prāk śreṣṭhāḥ sambhāravāhane ;
sarvebhyaḥ śakaṭāḥ śreṣṭhā varṣākālam vinā smṛtāḥ.
117. Na cālpasādhano gacchet api jetum ripum laghum
mahatātyantasādyaskabalenaiva subuddhiyuk.

---

111. and are joined with rings for reins both for stopping and pulling back ; with such a bridlebit one may manage a horse.

112. One may guide firmly a bull with a rein pulling through its nose, in cleaning them of dirt should be (used) an instrument with seven sharp-pointed combs. Bullrein.

113. Men and beasts should certainly always be managed by severe beating ; but soldiers specially ; they should not be subjected to fines.

114. By keeping horses and bulls in a marshy country, elephants in a jungle (and) foot-soldiers in a plain, their safety will be ensured.

115. At the end of each yojana,[145] a king should keep in his inhabited kingdom a troop of one hundred soldiers. Distribution of troops.

116. Elephants, camels, bulls and horses are in the order of precedence excellent for carrying provisions, better than all these are stated to be cars, except in the rainy season.

117. A wise general should not march even against a weak enemy insufficiently prepared, but only with a very numerous army consisting of troops of the line. Precepts on fighting and ruling.

---

[145] A *yojana* is a measure of different length, its shortest extent amounts to 2½ and its longest to about 18 English miles ; it is generally fixed at 4 krośas or 9 English miles.

118. Aśikṣitam asāram ca sādyaskam tūlavacca tat,
yuddham vinā'nyakāryeṣu yojayet matimān sadā.

119. Vikartum yatate'lpo'pi prāpte prāṇātyaye'niśam
na punaḥ kimtu balavān vikārakaraṇakṣamaḥ.

120. Apibahubalo'śūro na sthātum kṣamate raṇe
kim alpasādhano'śūraḥ sthātum śakto'riṇā samam?

121. Susiddhālpabalaśśūro vijetum kṣamate ripum,
mahāsusiddhabalayuk śūraḥ kim na vijeṣyati.

122. Maulaśikṣitasāreṇa gacchet rājā raṇe ripum
prāṇātyaye'pi maulam na svāminam tyaktum icchati.

123. Vāgdaṇḍaparuṣeṇaiva bhṛtihrāsena bhītitaḥ
nityam pravāsāyāsābhyām bhedo'vaśyam prajāyate.

---

118. An undisciplined and inefficient line is (weak) like cotton; a wise man should always apply it to all other purposes but fighting.

119. A weak person, if he is in danger of his life, tries always to fight, how much more a strong one, who is able to attack?

120. A coward though he has a very strong army cannot stand in the battle-field, how can a coward with small support stand in a battle?

121. A hero who has a small but well-disciplined army is able to conquer the enemy; (if so) will not a hero with a strong well-provided army conquer?

122. A king should go to battle against an enemy with an efficient and disciplined reserve, the reserve does not wish to leave his master even when in danger of death.

123. Discontent arises necessarily from severe reprimands and severe punishments, from fear, from reductions of pay, from always sojourning abroad and from fatigues.

124. Balam yasya tu sambhinnam manāk api jayaḥ kutaḥ
śatroḥ svasyāpi senāyā ato bhedam vicintayet.
125. Yathā hi śatrusenāyā bhedo'vaśyam bhavet tathā,
kauṭilyena pradānena drāk kuryāt nṛpatiḥ sadā.
126. Sevayātyantaprabalam natyā cārim prasādhayet
prabalam mānadānābhyām yuddhairhīnabalam tathā.
127. Maitryā jayet samabalam bhedaiḥ sarvān vaśam nayet,
śatrusaṁsādhanopāyo nānyaḥ subalabhedataḥ.
128. Tāvat paro nītimān syāt yāvat subalavān svayam
mitram tāvat ca bhavati puṣṭāgneḥ pavano yathā.
129. Tyaktam ripubalam dhāryam na samūhasamīpataḥ
pṛthak niyojayet prāk vā yuddhārtham kalpayet ca tat.

---

124. How can be victory to him, whose army is even a little discontented? he should therefore always investigate the discontent which exists in his army and in that of his enemy.

125. That discontent should necessarily prevail among the hostile army, a king should always speedily endeavour by deceitful means and bribes.

126. One should propitiate an overpowerful enemy by submission, a powerful one by demonstration of respect and by presents, and a weak one (one should subdue) by fighting.

Behaviour towards an enemy.

127. He should win over an equal in strength by friendship; by divisions he should subdue all. There is no other means of subduing an enemy than by (spreading) discontent among his strong army.

128. As long as an enemy is powerful he is able to govern, and so long he is a friend; as the wind is (a friend) of the strong fire.

129. The hostile army which has deserted to the king must be protected, but not kept near his own army; he should place it separately or arrange it in front for fighting.

130. Maitryam ārāt pṛṣṭhabhāge pārśvayorvā balam nyaset.

131. Asyate kṣipyate yat tu mantrayantrāgnibhiśca tat astram tadanyataḥ śastram asikuntādikam ca yat.

132. Astram tu dvividham jñeyam nālikam māntrikam tathā.

133. Yadā tu māntrikam nāsti nālikam tatra dhārayet saha śastreṇa nṛpatirvijayārtham tu sarvadā.

134. Laghudīrghākāradhārabhedaiḥ śastrāstranāmakam prathayanti navam bhinnam vyavahārāya tad vidaḥ.

135. Nālikam dvividham jñeyam bṛhatkṣudravibhedataḥ.

136. Tiryagūrdhvacchidramūlam nālam pañcavitastikam; mūlāgrayorlakṣyabheditilabinduyutam sadā.

---

130. He should place the friendly army near in the rear or on both sides.

131. Whatever is thrown or cast by incantation, machine or fire is a projectile, what is different is a weapon like the sword, the spear, &c. Projectiles and weapons.

132. The projectile weapon must be known to be of two kinds, that consisting of tubes and that thrown by incantation. Incantation arms, guns, and other weapons.

133. If here there are no incantation-arms a king should always keep for the sake of victory the tubular arms together with other weapons.

134. According as a new weapon and missile varies in its size, whether it is small or large, in its shape or blade, experts name it differently.

135. The tubular weapon should be known as being of two kinds, divided into large and small.

136. The tube is five spans long, its breech has a perpendicular and horizontal hole, at the breech and muzzle is always fixed a sesambead for aligning the sights. Gun.

137. Yantrāghātāgnikṛt grāvacūrṇadhṛk karṇamūlakam
sukāṣṭhopāṅgabudnam ca madhyaṅgulabilāntaram.

138. Svānte'gnicūrṇasandhātṛśalākāsaṁyutam dṛḍham
laghunālikam apyetat pradhāryam pattisādibhiḥ.

139. Yathā yathaitat tvaksāram yathā sthūlabilāntaram
yathā dīrghabṛhadgolam dūrabhedi tathā tathā.

140. Mūlakīlabhramāt lakṣyasamasandhānabhāji yat
bṛhannālīkasañjñam tat kāṣṭhabudhnavivarjitam
pravāhyam śakaṭādyaistu suyuktam vijayapradam.

141. Suvarcilavaṇāt pañca palāni gandhakāt palam
antardhūmavipakvārkasnuhyādyaṅgārataḥ palam ;

---

137. The breech has at the vent a mechanism which, carrying stone and powder, makes fire by striking. Its breech is well wooded at the side, in the middle is a hole an aṅgula broad ;

138. after the gunpowder is placed inside, it is firmly pressed down with a ramrod. This is the small gun which ought to be carried by foot-soldiers.

139. In proportion as its outside (bark) is hard, its hole is broad, its ball is long and broad ; the ball reaches far.

140. A big tube is called (that gun) which obtains the direction of the aim by moving the breech with a wedge ; its end is without wood ; but it is to be drawn on cars, &c. ; if well welded it gives victory.

141. Five weights (pala) of saltpetre, one weight of sulphur, one weight of charcoal, which consists of *Calatropis gigantea*, of *Euphorbia neriifolia*, and other (plants) and is prepared in such a manner that the smoke does not escape ; Gun-powder.

142. Śuddhāt saṅgrāhya sañcūrṇya sammīlya praputet rasaiḥ
snuhyarkāṇām rasonasya śoṣayet ātapena ca ;
piṣṭvā śarkaravat caitat agnicūrṇam bhavet khalu.
143. Suvarcilavaṇāt bhāgāḥ ṣaṭ vā catvāra eva vā
nālāstrārthāgnicūrṇe tu gandhāṅgārau tu pūrvavat.
144. Golo lohamayo garbhaguṭikaḥ kevalo'pi vā
sīsasya laghunālārthe hyanyadhātubhavo'pi vā.
145. Lohasāramayam vāpi nālāstram tvanyadhātujam
nityasammārjanasvaccham astrapātibhirāvṛtam.
146. Aṅgārasyaiva gandhasya suvarcilavaṇasya ca
śilāyā haritālasya tathā sīsamalasya ca.
147. Hiṅgulasya tathā kāntarajasaḥ karpurasya ca
jatornīlyāśca saralaniryāsasya tathaiva ca.

---

142. if all this is taken after having been cleansed, is then powdered, and mixed together, one should squeeze it with the juice of *Calatropis gigantea*, *Euphorbia neriifolia* and *Allium sativum* and dry in the sun ; having ground this like sugar, it will certainly become gunpowder.

143. There may be six or even four parts of saltpetre in the gunpowder used for tubular arms, but the parts of sulphur and charcoal remain as before.

144. The ball is made of iron, and has either small balls in its inside or is empty ; for small tubular arms it should be of lead or of any other metal.

145. The tubular projectile weapon is either of iron or of another metal, it is every day to be rubbed clean, and covered by gunners.

146. With a similar greater or less proportion of charcoal, sulphur, and saltpetre, of realgar, of opiment and likewise of graphite ;

147. of vermilion, also of powder of magnetic iron oxide and of camphor, of lac, and of indigo and likewise of the pine gum (*Pinus longifolia*),

148. Samanyūnādhikhairaṁśairagnicūrṇānyanekaśaḥ
kalpayanti ca vettāraḥ candrikābhādimanti ca.

149. Kṣipanti cāgnisaṁyogāt golam lakṣe sunālagam.

150. Nālāstram śodhayet ādau dadyāt tatrāgnicūrṇakam ;
niveśayet tat daṇḍena nālamūle yathā dṛḍham.

151. Tataḥ sugolakam dadyāt tataḥ karṇe'gnicūrṇakam,
karṇacūrṇāgnidānena golam lakṣye nipātayet.

152. Lakṣyabhedī yathā bāṇo dhanurjyāviniyojitaḥ
bhavet tathānusandhāya dvihastaśca śilīmukhaḥ.

153. Aṣṭāśrā pṛthubudhnā tu gadā hṛdayasaṁhitā ;
paṭṭiśaḥ svasamo hastabudhnaścobhayatomukhaḥ.

---

148. experts make gunpowder in many ways and of white and other colours.

149. By the application of fire they throw the ball coming from the tube at the mark. Gun-ball.

150. One should clean the tube first and then put gunpowder, carry it down with the ramrod to the bottom of the tube till it is tight, About loading and cleaning a gun.

151. then put a good ball, and place gunpowder on the vent, and by setting fire to the powder at the vent discharge the ball towards its mark.

152. In order that the arrow despatched by the string of the bow should penetrate the object aimed at, the arrow which is put on should be two cubits long. Bow, arrow.

153. A club is octagonal, but broad at the end, rising (from the ground) up to the heart; a battle axe is of the same height (as the bearer), is in the middle one cubit broad and is double-headed. Club. Battle axe.

154. Īṣadvaktraścaikadhāro vistāre caturaṅgulaḥ
kṣuraprānto nābhisamo dṛḍhamuṣṭissucandraruk
khaḍgaḥ, prāsaścaturhastadaṇḍabudhnaḥ kṣurānanaḥ.
155. Daśahastamitaḥ kuntaḥ phālāgraḥ śaṅkubudhnakaḥ.
156. Cakram ṣaḍhastaparidhi kṣuraprāntam sunābhiyuk,
trihastadaṇḍaḥ triśikho, loharajjuḥ supāśakaḥ.
157. Godhūmasaṁhitasthūlapatram lohamayam dṛḍham,
kavacam saśirastrāṇam ūrdhvakāyaviśobhanam.
158. Tīkṣṇāgram karajam śreṣṭham lohasāramayam dṛḍham.
159. Yo vai supuṣṭasambhāraḥ tathā ṣaḍguṇamantravit
bahvastrasaṁyuto rājā yoddhum icchet sa eva hi,
anyathā duḥkham āpnoti svarājyāt bhraśyate' pi ca.

---

154. The sword is a little curved, has one blade, is four aṅgulas broad, at the point sharp as a razor, reaches up to the navel, has a strong hilt and is as brilliant as the beautiful moon. The broad sword is four cubits long, broad (at the hilt), and at the end-point sharp like a razor. **Sword.** **Broad sword.**

155. The lance is ten cubits long, ending in a (metal) point, and broad as a shaft. **Lance.**

156. The disk is six cubits in circumference, is at the edge like a razor and is to be handled in the very midst; the trident is three cubits long; a good lasso has iron strings. **Disk.** **Trident.** **Lasso.**

157. Armour consists of scales of the breadth of a grain of wheat, is of metal and firm, has a protection for the head, and is ornamented on the upper part of the body. **Armour.**

158. The fingertip of a gauntlet which is sharp at its end, is of metal and is strong, is surely the best. **Gauntlet.**

159. That king who has well supplied provisions, knows the secret of the six principles of policy (*see* śl. 174), and has many weapons, wishes certainly to fight; if he is not in such position (and fights), he experiences distress, and is even expelled from his kingdom. **Rules about fighting.**

160. Ābibhratoḥ śatrubhāvam ubhayoḥ saṁyatātmanoḥ astrādyaiḥ svārthasiddhyartham vyāpāro yuddham ucyate.
161. Mantrāstrairdaivikam yuddham, nālādyaiśca tathā 'suram
śastrabāhusamuttham tu mānavam yuddham īritam.
162. Ekasya bahubhiḥ sārddham bahūnām bahubhiśca vā
ekasyaikena vā, dvābhyām dvayor vā, tat bhavet khalu.
163 Kālam deśam śatrubalam dṛṣṭvā svīyabalam tataḥ
upāyān ṣaḍguṇam mantram sambhūyāt yuddhakāmukaḥ.
164. Śaraddhemantaśiśirakālo yuddheṣu cottamaḥ
vasanto madhyamo jñeyo'dhamo grīṣmaḥ smṛtaḥ sadā.
165. Varṣāsu na praśaṁsanti yuddham sāma smṛtam tadā.

Definition of war.

160. The exertion of two self-controlled (parties) who harbour enmity against each other with projectile weapons and other arms for the accomplishment of their own benefit, is called war.

Different mode of fighting.

161. The fighting with incantations and projectile weapons is called divine, that with tubes and other instruments demoniac, that with weapons and the arms (of the body) is human.

162. If one fights with many, or many fight against many, or one fights against one, or two against two, that is surely a contest.

163. Having considered the time, place, the hostile army and also his own, the (four) expedients (*i.e.*, negotiation, bribery, dissension and attack), the secret of the six principles of policy, he should think of war.

Seasons of the year to be considered.

164. Autumn, winter and the chilly season are the best for fighting, spring time should be regarded as middling, and the hot season always as the worst.

165. In the rainy season they do not recommend war; for that time negotiation is advised.

166. Yuddhasambhārasampanno yadādhikabalo nṛpaḥ
manotsāhī suśakunotpātī kālaḥ tadā śubhaḥ.

167. Kārye'tyavaśyake prāpte kālo no cet yadā śubhaḥ
nidhāya hṛdi viśveśam gehe cihnam iyāt tadā.

168. Na kālaniyamaḥ tatra gostrīvipravināśane.

169. Yasmin deśe yathākālaṁ sainyavyāyāmabhūmayaḥ
parasya viparītāśca smṛto deśaḥ sa uttamaḥ.[146]

170. Ātmanaśca pareṣām ca tulyavyāyāmabhūmayaḥ
yatra madhyama uddiṣṭo deśaḥ śāstravicintakaiḥ.[147]

---

166. When a king has acquired all war materials, is very strong, persevering in his mind, (and) has obtained auspicious omens, then is the time.

167. But if the business is unavoidable, and the time is not propitious, he should go, after having meditated in his mind on the Supreme Spirit and placed a (divine) symbol in his house.

Unavoidable war to be accepted.

168. There is no restriction as to time (for fighting) when cows, women, and Brahmans are being destroyed.

169. That position in which there are at the necessary time fields fit for the manœuvring of troops, the position of the enemy being in this respect different, is mentioned as the best.

Manœuvring.

170. If his own good manœuvring fields and those of his enemies are equally good, the position is called a middling one by war experts.

---

[146] *See* Kāmandakīya, XVI, 19.

[147] *See* Kāmand., XVI, 20.
Ātmanaśca pareṣām ca tulyā vyāyāmabhūmayaḥ
sumadhyamaḥ sa uddiṣṭo deśaḥ śastrārthacintakaiḥ.

171. Arātisainyavyāyāmasuparyāptamahītalaḥ
ātmano viparītaśca sa vai deśo'dhamaḥ smṛtaḥ.[148]

172. Svasainyāt tu tritīyāṁśahīnam śatrubalam yadi
aśikṣitam asāram vā sādyaskam svajayāya vai.

173. Putravat pālitam yat tu dānamānavivarddhitam
yuddhasambhārasampannam svasainyam vijayapradam.

174. Sandhim ca vigraham yānam āsanam ca samāśrayam
dvaidhībhāvam ca saṁvidyāt mantrasyaitānstu ṣaḍguṇān

175. Yābhiḥ kriyābhiḥ balavān mitratām yāti vai ripuḥ
sā kriyā sandhirityuktā vimṛśet tām tu yatnataḥ.

176. Vikarṣitaḥ san vādhīno bhavet śatrustu yena vai
karmaṇā vigraham tam tu cintayet mantribhirnṛpaḥ.

---

171. If the ground is favorable for the manœuvres of the army of the enemy, his position being quite the reverse, that position is mentioned as the worst.

172. If the hostile army is a third part less than his own, if its line is undisciplined and inefficient, (such circumstances) ensure his own victory.

173. If his own army is guarded like a son, is gratified by presents and honours, is provided with the materials for war, it is conferring victory.

Six principles of policy.

174. He should understand the six principles of policy; alliance and quarrel, marching, halting, refuge and separation.

Alliance.

175. By what practices a strong enemy is won over to friendship, that practice is called alliance; he should consider it anxiously.

War.

176. A king should deliberate with his ministers about the war, by means of which his enemy may be injured and rendered dependent.

---

[148] *See* Kāmand., XVI, 21.

177. Śatrunāśārthagamanam yānam svābhīṣṭasiddhaye
svarakṣaṇam śatrunāśo bhavet sthānāt tadāsanam.

178. Yairgupto balavān bhūyāt durbalo'pi sa āśrayaḥ,
dvaidhībhāvaḥ svasainyānām sthāpanam gulmagulmataḥ.

179. Balīyasābhiyuktastu nṛpo'nanyapratikriyaḥ
āpannaḥ sandhim anvicchet kurvāṇaḥ kālayāpanam.

180. Eka evopahārastu sandhireṣa mato hitaḥ,
upahārasya bhedāstu sarve'nye maitravarjitāḥ.[149]

181. Abhiyoktā balīyastvāt alabdhvā na nivartate
upahārādṛte yasmāt sandhiranyo na vidyate.[150]

---

177. The going for the destruction of the enemy for the fulfilment of his own desires is marching; if through staying his own safety and his enemy's destruction is obtained, that is halting. Marching. Halting.

178. The protection which makes a weak man become strong, is called refuge; the placing of his own armies in different corps is separation. Refuge. Separation.

179. If a king is attacked by a strong enemy and is not able to resist, he should (thus) afflicted make peace, obtaining delay of time. Political advice.

180. Alliance alone is regarded as a pleasant tribute; but all the other kinds of tributes are destitute of friendship.

181. As an enemy who has not received any benefit from his superior strength does not return (to his country); therefore no peace is known without a tribute.

---

[149] *See* Kāmand., IX, 21, and Hitopadeśa, IV, 126.

[150] *See* Kāmand., IX, 22.
Abhiyoktā balī yasmāt alabdhvā na nivartate
upahārāt ṛte tasmāt sandhiranyo na vidyate.

182. Śatrorbalānusāreṇa upahāram prakalpayet
sevām vāpi ca svīkuryāt dadyāt kanyām .bhuvam dhanam.
183. Svasāmantāñśca sandhīyāt maitreṇānyajayāya vai
sandhiḥ kāryo'pyanāryeṇa samprāpyotsādayet hi saḥ.
184. Saṅghātavān yathā veṇurnividaiḥ kaṇṭakairvṛtaḥ
na śakyate samucchettum veṇuḥ saṅghātavānstathā.[151]
185. Balinā saha sandhāya bhaye sādhāraṇe yadi,
ātmānam gopayet kāle bahvamitreṣu buddhimān.
186. Balinā saha yoddhavyam iti nāsti nidarśanam
prativātam hi na ghanaḥ kadācit api sarpati.[152]

---

182. He should settle a tribute according to the strength of his enemy, or he should agree to do homage, or should give his daughter, land or money.

183. For the sake of conquering his enemy he should make an alliance with his neighbours; an alliance is even to be made with an unworthy ruler; having gained his object he may destroy him.

184. As a clump of bamboos surrounded by thick thorns cannot be torn out, thus also could not be annihilated Veṇu (?) who had a multitude of followers.

185. A wise king who has many enemies should guard himself in calamity by making an alliance with a strong king, who is exposed to the same danger.

186. There exists no example (to show), that one should fight with a strong enemy; a cloud surely does not move against the wind.

---

[151] *See* Hitop., IV, 26.
Saṁhatatvāt yathā Veṇurnividaḥ kaṇṭakairvṛtaḥ
na śakyate samucchettum bhrātṛsaṅghātavānstathā.
Pañc., III, 50. Saṅghātavān yathā veṇurnivido veṇubhirvṛtaḥ
na śakyate samucchettum durbalopi tathā nṛpaḥ.
Kāmandakīya, IX, 46.
Saṅghātavān yathā veṇurnividaiḥ kaṇṭakair vṛtaḥ
na śakyate samucchettum bhrātṛsaṅghātavānstathā.
All MSS. of the Śukranīti read *Veṇuḥ saṅghātavānstathā.*

[152] *See* Hitop., IV, 27; Pañcatantra, III, 22; Kāmandakīya, III, 46.

187. Balīyasi praṇamatām kāle vikramatām api
sampado na visarpanti pratīpam iva nimnagāḥ.
188. Rājā na gacchet viśvāsam sandhito' pi hi buddhimān
adrohasamayam kṛtvā vṛtram indraḥ purā'vadhīt.[153]
189. Āpanno' bhyudayākāṅkṣī pīḍyamānaḥ pareṇa vā
deśakālabalopetaḥ prārabheta ca vigraham.
190. Prahīnabalamitram tu durgastham hyantarāgatam
atyantaviṣayāsaktam prajādravyāpahārakam;
bhinnamantribalam rājā pīḍayet pariveṣṭayan.
191. Vigrahaḥ sa ca vijñeyo hyanyaśca kalahaḥ smṛtaḥ.
192. Balīyasātyalpabalaḥ śūreṇa na ca vigraham
kuryāt ca vigrahe puṁsām sarvanāśaḥ prajāyate.

---

187. The power of those kings, who bow to a strong enemy, but fight at another time, does not glide away, as rivers do not flow against the stream.

188. A wise king does not enter into confidence even if he has made an alliance; Indra after having made friendship killed in ancient times Vṛtra.

189. When unfortunate, or hoping for success, or troubled by an enemy, one should commence war only, after having obtained the (right) place, time and army.

190. A king should beleaguer and oppress an enemy who is deficient in army and in friends, who stays in his fortress, who has invaded his country, who is much addicted to women, who robs his subjects of their money, and whose ministers and army are disaffected.

191. This is regarded as war, but a quarrel is regarded as a different thing.

192. A very weak one should not go to war with a strong enemy, for in such a combat of men occurs general destruction.

---

[153] *See* Pañc., III. 7; Kāmand., IX. 50 to śloka 187; and Kāmand., IX. 53 to śloka 188.

193. Ekārthābhiniveśitvam kāraṇam kalahasya vā
upāyāntaranāśe tu tato vigraham ācaret.
194. Vigṛhya sandhāya tathā sambhūyātha prasaṅgataḥ
upekṣayā ca nipuṇairyānam pañcavidham smṛtam.[154]
195. Vigṛhya yāti hi yadā sarvān śatrugaṇān balāt
vigṛhya yānam yānajñaiḥ tadācāryaiḥ pracakṣyate.[155]
196. Arimitrāṇi sarvāṇi svamitraiḥ sarvato balāt
vigṛhya cāribhirgantum vigṛhyagamanam tu vā.[156]
197. Sandhāyānyatra yātrāyām pārṣṇigrāheṇa śatruṇā
sandhāyagamanam proktam tajjigīṣoḥ phalārthinaḥ.[157]

---

193. If the cause of the quarrel is the desire to have one and the same object, one may proceed to war, if no other means exists (to settle the matter).

194. Five different modes of marching are mentioned by experts, a successful war march, an alliance march, a junction march, likewise an incidental march, and a contemptuous march. Marching.

195. If by his strength all hostile troops are conquered, it is called by the masters who know the marching rules, a successful war march.

196. If, when marching against one's own enemies, all the friends of the enemy are everywhere conquered through the ability of one's own friends, this is also called a successful war expedition.

197. When, while marching against one enemy, an alliance is made with another enemy, who is coming in his rear, this is called the alliance march of the king desirous success.

---

[154] *See* Kāmand., XI, 2, instead of *upekṣayā ca* upekṣā ceti.

[155] *See* Kāmand., XI, 3.

[156] *See* Kāmand., XI, 4, instead of *ari* arer, and instead of *cāribhirgantum* "cābhigamanam."

[157] *See* Kāmand., XI, 5.

198. Eko bhūpo yadaikatra sāmantaiḥ sāmparāyikaiḥ
śaktiśauryayutairyānam sambhūyagamanam hi tat.[158]

199. Anyatra prasthitaḥ saṅgāt anyatraiva ca gacchati
prasaṅgayānam tat proktam yānavidbhiśca mantribhiḥ.[159]

200. Ripum yātasya balinaḥ samprāpya vikṛtam phalam
upekṣya tasmin tadyānam upekṣāyānam ucyate.[160]

201. Durvṛtte' pyakulīne tu balam dātari rajyate
hṛṣṭam kṛtvā svīyabalam paritoṣyapradānataḥ.

---

198. If a king marches against an enemy together with his warlike, powerful and valiant neighbours, that is called going together.

199. If, after having set out against one enemy, he marches by circumstances (compelled) against another enemy, this is called by those who understand marching and by ministers, an incidental march.

200. If, when a strong king marches against an (insignificant) enemy, an advantage not worth having has been obtained and this has been given up, this is called a march conducted with contempt.

201. An army is even attached to a bad and low born king if he is only liberal, having pleased his own army by gifts of presents. Liberality towards troops.

---

[158] *Compare* Kāmandakīya, XI, 6.
Ekībhūya yadaikatra sāmantaiḥ sāmparāyikaiḥ
śaktiśaucayutairyānam sambhūyagamanam hi tat.

[159] *Compare* Kāmandakīya, XI, 9.
Anyatra prasthitaḥ saṅgāt anyatraiva ca gacchati
prasaṅgayānam tat proktam atra śalyo nidarśanam.

[160] *Compare* Kāmandakīya, XI, 10.
Ripum yātasya balinaḥ samprāpyāviṣkṛtam phalam
upekṣya tanmitrayānam upekṣāyānam ucyate.

202. Nāyakaḥ purato yāyāt pravīrapuruṣāvṛtaḥ
madhye kalatram kośaśca svāmī phalguca yaddhanam,[161]
dhvajinīm ca sadodyuktaḥ sa gopayet divāniśam.[162]
203. Nadyadrivanadurgeṣu yatra yatra bhayam bhavet
senāpatiḥ tatra tatra gacchet vyūhīkṛtairbalaiḥ.[163]
204. Yāyāt vyuhena mahatā makareṇa purobhaye;
śyenenobhayapakṣeṇa sūcyā vā dhīravaktrayā.[164]
205. Paścādbhaye tu śakaṭam pārśvayorvajrasañjñikam
sarvataḥ sarvatobhadram cakram vyālam athāpi vā;[165]
yathādeśam kalpayet vā śatrusenāvibhedakam.
206. Vyūharacanasaṅketān vādyabhāṣāsamīritān

---

202. The commander-in-chief should go in front, surrounded by valiant men, in the midst should be the queen, the treasury, the king, and whatever ready money there is; and he should always zealously guard his army day and night.

203. Wherever, whether in a river, mountain, forest or fortress an alarm of the enemy (coming) arises, there should the general go with combined forces.

204. If the alarm arises in front, he should march in an array resembling a crocodile, a double-winged hawk or a needle with a strong point. *Different formations of troops.*

205. A king should form if the alarm rises in the rear what is called a cart, if on the flanks a thunderbolt, if on all sides, an everywhere impregnable figure, a wheel and an elephant for the destruction of the hostile army according to the fitness of the place.

206. No body except his own soldiers should know the intima- *Signals.*

---

[161] *See* Hit., III, 70; Kamand., XVIII, 45.
Nāyakaḥ purato yāyāt pravīrapṛtanāvṛtah
madhye kalatram svāmī ca kośaḥ phalgu mahaddhanam.

[162] *See* Kāmandakīya, XVIII, 43.

[163] *See* Kāmand., XVIII, 44; Hitop., III, 69; and compare Manu, VII, 188.

[164] *See* Kāmand., XVIII, 48.

[165] *See* Kāmand., XVIII, 49.
Paścādbhaye tu śakaṭam pārśvayorvajrasañjñitam
sarvataḥ sarvatobhadram bhayavyūham prakalpayet.

svasainikairvinā kopi na jānāti tathāvidhān,
niyojayet ca matimān vyūhān nānāvidhān sadā.

207. Aśvānām ca gajānām ca padātīnām pṛthak pṛthak
uccaiḥ saṁśrāvayet vyūhasaṅketān sainikān nṛpaḥ.

208. Vāmadakṣiṇasaṁstho vā madhyastho vāgrasaṁsthitaḥ
śrutvā tān sainikaiḥ kāryam anuśiṣṭam yathā tathā.

209. Sammīlanam prasaraṇam paribhramaṇam eva ca
ākuñcanam tathā yānam prayāṇam apayānakam;

210. Paryāyeṇa ca sāmmukhyam samutthānam ca luṇṭhanam
saṁsthānam cāṣṭadalavat cakravat golatulyakam;

211. Sūcītulyam śakaṭavat ardhacandrasamam tu vā
pṛthagbhavanam alpālpaiḥ paryāyaiḥ paṅktiveśanam;

212. Śastrāstrayordhāraṇam ca sandhānam lakṣyabhedanam
mokṣaṇam ca tathāstrāṇām śastrāṇām parighātanam.

---

tions for the arrangement of troops, communicated by words or signals; and a wise man should always prescribe different formations.

207. A king should make his soldiers hear distinctly the formation-signals for the elephants, horses and foot-soldiers each separately;

208. whether he stands on the left or right, in the midst or is placed in front; the soldiers, when they hear these signals, should do according as they are taught.

209. They should concentrate, spread, wheel round, fall in, march, double and retreat; Manœuvres.

210. now face or rise and lie down on the ground, or stand like an octagon, like a wheel, like a ball;

211. like a needle, like a car, or like the halfmoon, skirmish in small numbers, form rows in regular order;

212. take up weapons and arms, aim at and hit the mark, discharge missiles and strike with weapons,

213. Drāk sandhānam punaḥ pāto graho mokṣaḥ punaḥ punaḥ;
svagūhanam pratīghātaḥ śastrāstrapadavikramaiḥ.
214. Dvābhyām tribhiścaturbhirvā paṅktiśo gamanam tataḥ;
tathā prāgbhavanam cāpasaraṇam tūpasarjanam
apasṛtyāstrasiddhyartham upasṛtya vimokṣaṇam.
215. Prāgbhūtvā mocayet astram vyūhasthaḥ sainikaḥ sadā
āsīnaḥ syāt vimuktāstraḥ prāgvā cāpasaret punaḥ.
216. Prāgāsīnam tūpasṛto dṛṣṭvā svāstram vimocayet
ekaikaśo dviśo vāpi saṅghaśo bodhito yathā.
217. Krauñcānām khe gatiryādṛk paṅktitaḥ samprajāyate
tādṛk saṁrakṣayet krauñcavyūham deśabalam yathā,
218. Sūkṣmagrīvam madhyapuccham sthūlapakṣam tu paṅktitaḥ
bṛhatpakṣam madhyagalapuccham śyenam mukhe tanum.

---

213. then quickly aim again, and throw, take up and discharge the arms repeatedly, cover themselves, and beat with arms, weapons and feet;

214. further go in rows of two, three or four; likewise, front, retire and change places; retire for adjusting the arms and advance for the discharge.

215. A soldier when standing in his corps should always discharge his arms from the front, if he has discharged the arms he should sit down, or should leave the front.

216. But (the next soldier) advancing should discharge his weapon keeping his eye on him who sits in front, either one by one, or in twos or in numbers, according to the order.

217. As the moving of the herons proceeds in the sky, he should arrange the herons' array, according as it is adapted to the country; Formation of troops.

218. with a thin neck, a middling tail, a bulky wing, arranged

219. Catuṣpād makaro dīrghasthūlavakro dviroṣṭhakaḥ
sūcī sūkṣmamukho dīrghasamadaṇḍāntarandhrayuk.
220. Cakravyūhaḥ caikamārgo hyaṣṭadhā kuṇḍalīkṛtaḥ
caturdikṣvaṣṭaparidhiḥ sarvatobhadrasañjñikaḥ.
221. Amārgaścāṣṭavalayī golakaḥ sarvatomukhaḥ
śakaṭaḥ śakaṭākāro vyālo vyālākṛtiḥ sadā.
222. Sainyam alpam bṛhadvāpi dṛṣṭvā mārgam raṇasthalam
vyūhairvyūhena vyūhābhyām saṅkareṇāpi kalpayet.
223. Yantrāstraiḥ śatrusenāyā bhedo yebhyaḥ prajāyate,
sthalebhyasteṣu santiṣṭhet sasaīnyo hyāsanam hi tat.
224. Tṛṇānnajalasambhārā ye cānye śatrupoṣakāḥ
saṁyak nirudhya tān yatnāt paritaściram āsanāt.

---

in rows, (and) a hawk-array with a broad wing, a middling throat and tail and thin at the face.

219. The crocodile has four feet, a long and broad snout and two lips. A needle has a thin face, a long and even stick-like body, and a hole at its end.

220. The wheel array has one way, but eight coils. A figure with eight rings and with four faces is called a *Sarvatobhadra* (a strong one on every direction).

221. A ball has no entrance, eight circles and everywhere a face ; a cart is like a cart and an elephant has always the shape of an elephant.

222. Having seen the army, the road, the battlefield, whether small or big, he should arrange his army in many corps, or in one or two, or in one mass.

223. Where a gap may be made in the hostile army through Post.
missiles and machines, in these places the king should stand with his army ; this is called post.

224. Having with great exertion effectually removed from his post all round and for a long time to come grass, food, water and other provisions, which maintain the enemy ;

225. Vicchinnavividhāsāram prakṣīṇayavasaindhanam,
vigṛhyamāṇaprakṛtim kālenaiva vaśam nayet.[166]
226. Areśca vijigīṣośca vigrahe hīyamānayoḥ
sandhāya yadavasthānam sandhāyāsanam ucyate.[167]
227. Ucchidyamāno balinā nirupāyapratikriyaḥ,
kulodbhavam satyam āryam āśrayeta balotkaṭam.
228. Vijigīṣostu sāhyārthāḥ suhṛtsambandhibāndhavāḥ
pradattabhṛtikā hyanye bhūpā aṁśaprakalpitāḥ.
229. Saivāśrayastu kathito durgāṇi ca mahātmabhiḥ.
230. Aniścitopāyakāryaḥ samayānucaro nṛpaḥ
dvaidhībhāvena varteta kākākṣivat alakṣitam,[168]
pradarśayet anyakāryam anyam ālambayet ca vā.

---

225. he should subdue in time the enemy, whose various provisions are scattered, whose corn and fuel is destroyed and whose subjects are incensed.

226. If the enemy and the king who wishes to conquer are reduced in the war, the place where they stand, when they make peace, is called the place produced by peace.

227. If a king who has no means of redress is much oppressed by a strong king he should take refuge with a king, who is well-born, righteous, venerable and of superior strength. **Refuge.**

228. A king (who wishes to conquer) has friends, connections and relations who assist for the sake of friendship, others who have received pay, and kings on whom is settled a part (of the enemy's country).

229. By great-minded men this is surely called refuge and a fortress is also called a refuge.

230. A king, whose arrangements are not certain, looking out for the opportune time, should practise duplicity like the concealed eye of a crow, he should pretend one thing and seize another. **Duplicity.**

---

[166] *See* Kāmand., XI, 16. [167] *See* Kāmand., XI, 17.
[168] *See* Kāmand., XI, 24b.

231. Sadupāyaiśca sanmantraiḥ kāryasiddhirathodyamaiḥ
bhavet alpajanasyāpi kim punarnṛpaterna hi.
232. Udyogenaiva siddhyanti kāryāṇi na manorathaiḥ.
233. Na hi suptamṛgendrasya nipatanti gajā mukhe[169];
ayo'bhedyam upāyena dravatām upanīyate.[170]
234. Lokaprasiddham evaitat vāri vahnerniyāmakam
upāyopagṛhītena tenaitat pariśoṣyate.[171]
235. Upāyena padam mūrdhni nyasyate mattahastinām[172]
upāyeṣūttamo bhedaḥ sadguṇeṣu samāśrayaḥ.
236. Kāryau dvau sarvadā tau tu nṛpeṇa vijigīṣuṇā,
tābhyām vinā naiva kuryāt yuddham rājā kadācana.

---

231. The success of the undertaking of even an insignificant man may be ensured by clever stratagems, good councils and efforts, would this not be surely the case with a king?

Necessity of exerting oneself.

232. Undertakings really succeed by efforts alone and not by wishes.

233. Elephants certainly do not fall into the mouth of the sleeping lion. The iron which cannot be broken is brought by expedients to fluidity.

234. That the water is the subduer of the fire is surely well known in the world, but it is dried up by that fire if assisted by proper means.

235. The foot is placed on the wild elephant by stratagem. Among all expedients the division of friends is the best; amongst the six principles of policy the refuge is the best.

236. These two ought always to be used by a king who wishes to conquer; without these two no king could ever undertake a war.

---

169 *See* Hitop., 1, 36b.
na hi suptasya siṁhasya praviśanti mukhe mṛgāḥ.

170 *See* Kāmand., XI, 47b.

171 *See* Kāmand., XI, 49. *tenaiva* instead of *tenaitat*.

172 *See* Kāmand., XI, 46b.

237. Parasparam prātikūlyam ripusenāpamantriṇām,
bhavet yathā tathā kuryāt tat prajāyāśca tat striyaḥ.

238. Upāyān ṣaḍguṇān vīkṣya śatroḥ svasyāpi sarvadā,
yuddham prāṇātyaye kuryāt sarvasvaharaṇe sati.

239. Strīviprābhyupapattau ca govināśepi brāhmaṇaiḥ,
prāpte yuddhe kvacinnaiva bhavet api parāṅmukhaḥ.

240. Yuddham utsṛjya yo yāti sa devairhanyate bhṛśam.

241. Samottamādhamai rājā tvāhūtaḥ pālayan prajāḥ,
na nivarteta saṅgrāmāt kṣatradharmam anusmaran.[173]

242. Rājānam cāpayoddhāram brāhmaṇam cāpravāsinam,
nirgilati bhūmiretau sarpo vilaśayān iva.[174]

General political advice.

237. He should contrive so that there is mutual enmity among the ministers and generals of the enemy and also among the subjects and women.

238. In case his life is in danger, or all his property is to be taken, he should fight having always considered the six-fold expedients of his enemy and of himself.

239. If he has undertaken the war for the defence of women and Brahmans and on account of the destruction of cows even if done by Brahmans, he should never turn away.

240. Who goes away having left the fight is quickly destroyed by the gods.

241. A king who protects his subjects if he is summoned to fight by equal, superior, or inferior enemies should not turn from the contest remembering the duty of a Kṣatriya.

242. A king who does not fight and a Brahman who does not travel about; these two swallows the earth, like a snake doės the animals living in holes.

---

[173] *See* Manu, VII, 87.

[174] *See* Mahabhārata, Rājadharma, LVII, 1, and the observations on this śloka on pp. 38 and 39.

243. Brāhmaṇasyāpi cāpattau kṣatradharmeṇa vartataḥ,
praśastam jīvitam loke kṣatram hi brahmasambhavam.

244. Adharmaḥ kṣatriyasyaiṣa yacchayyāmaraṇam bhavet,
visṛjan śleṣmapittāni kṛpaṇam paridevayan.[175]

245. Avikṣatena dehena pralayam yo' dhigacchati
kṣatriyo nāsya tat karma praśaṁsanti purāvidaḥ.[176]

246. Na gṛhe maraṇam śastam kṣatriyāṇām vinā raṇāt,
śauṇḍīrāṇām aśauṇḍīram adharmam kṛpaṇam hi yat.[177]

247. Raṇeṣu kadanam kṛtvā jñātibhiḥ parivāritaḥ
śastrāstraiḥ suvinirbhinnaḥ kṣatriyo vadham arhati.[178]

Prescriptions for Kṣatriyas.

243. Even for a Brahman who lives during misfortune according to the Kṣatriya rule, it is in the world a laudable living, for a Kṣatriya is sprung from Brahma.

244. There would be a demerit to a Kṣatriya whose death would be on a couch, emitting phlegm and bile and wailing piteously.

245. Those persons who are acquainted with the past do not praise the death of that Kṣatriya who meets his dissolution with unwounded body.

246. The death of Kṣatriyas in a house without a combat is not praised; it would be despicable, unrighteous, and miserable.

247. A Kṣatriya has earned (a noble) death, when, surrounded by his relations, he has made a slaughter (of enemies) on the battle fields, and is well pierced with arms and missiles.

---

[175] *See* Mahābhārata, Śāntiparva, Rājadharma, XCVII, 23.

[176] *See* Mahābhārata, Śāntiparva, Rājadharma, XCVII, 24.

[177] *See* ibidem, 25; instead of *śastam* tāta, and instead of *vinā raṇāt* praśasyate.

[178] *See* ibidem, 28; but the second half of the śloka differs, for instead of it we read *tīkṣṇaiḥ śastrairabhikliṣṭaḥ kṣatriyo mṛtyum arhati.* The change in the reading *tīkṣṇaiḥ śastraiḥ* for *śastrāstraiḥ* is significant.

248. Āhaveṣu mitho'nyonyam jighāṁsanto mahīkṣitaḥ
yudhyamānāḥ param śaktyā svargam yāntyaparāṅmukhāḥ.[179]

249. Bharturartheca yaḥ śūro vikramet vāhinīmukhe
bhayāt na nivarteta tasya svargo hyanantakaḥ.

250. Āhave nihatam śūram na śoceta kadācana[180]
nirmuktaḥ sarvapāpebhyaḥ pūto yāti salokatām.

251. Varāpsarassahasrāṇi śūram āyodhane hatam
tvaramāṇāḥ pradhāvanti hyayam mama bhavet iti.[181]

252. Munibhirdīrghatapasā prāpyate yat padam mahat
yuddhābhimukhanihataiḥ śūraiḥ tat drāk avāpyate.

253. Etat tapaśca puṇyam ca dharmaścaiva sanātanaḥ
catvāra āśramāstasya yo yuddhe na palāyate.[182]

---

248. The rulers of the earth, who, wishing to kill each other in battles, are fighting with utmost strength, go to heaven with not averted heads.

249. That hero who fights for the sake of his king in front of the army, nor turns away from fear, is sure of the everlasting heaven.

250. One should never bewail a hero who is killed in battle, freed from all sins he goes purified to the world specially assigned to him.

251. Towards a hero who is killed in battle run thousands of the best Apsaras, saying: "this one should be mine."

252. That grand step which after long penance is obtained by sages, is quickly won by heroes, who are killed with their faces turned towards the contest.

253. He who does not run away in the battle, earns this penance, this merit, this primeval virtue and the four stages.

---

179 *See* Manu, VII, 89; and Nītiprakāśikā, VII, 44.

180 *Compare* Mahābhārata, Rajadharma, XCVIII, 43b.

181 *See* Parāśarasmṛti, IV, 37; and Mahābhārata, ibidem, XCVIII, 45b and 46a; the latter half śloka runs there thus: tvaramāṇābhidhavanti mama bhartā bhavet iti.

182 *See* Mahābhārata, ibidem XCVIII, 46b and 47a.

254. Na hi śauryāt param kiñcit triṣu lokeṣu vidyate
śūraḥ sarvam pālayati śure sarvam pratiṣṭhitam.[183]

255. Carāṇām acarā annam adaṁṣṭrā daṁṣṭriṇām api
apāṇayaḥ pāṇimatām annam śūrasya kātarāḥ.[184]

256. Dvāvimau puruṣau loke sūryamaṇḍalabhedinau
parivrāṭ yogayuktaśca raṇe cābhimukho hataḥ.[185]

257. Ātmānam gopayet śakto vadhenāpyātatāyinaḥ,
suvidyabrāhmaṇaguroryuddhe śrutinidarśanāt.

258. Ātatāyitvam āpanno brāhmaṇaḥ śūdravat smṛtaḥ
nātatāyivadhe doṣo hanturbhavati kaścana.[186]

---

254. In the three worlds there is nothing known better than heroism, the hero protects all, in a hero all is fixed.

255. The food of moving beings is the immoveable, of those who have fangs those that have no fangs, of those who have hands those who have no hands; the food of the hero is the coward.

256. These two persons in the world have penetrated to the sphere of the sun, the devotee who is immersed in deep meditation, and he who is killed, whilst turned to the battle.

257. A strong man may according to the order of the Veda protect himself in the battle by slaying a preceptor, who is a learned Brahman, if he attempts his life.

When a Brahman-murder allowed.

258. A Brahman who has committed a murder is regarded as a Śūdra; for the murder of an assassin no fault whatever is to be found with the person who kills him.

---

183 *See* Mahabhārata, ibidem, XCIX, 18.

184 *See* Mahābhārata, ibidem, XCIX, 15.
Carāṇām acarā hyannam adaṁṣṭrā daṁṣṭriṇām api
apaḥ pipāsatām annam annam śūrasya kātarāḥ.

185 *See* Parāśarasmṛti, IV, 32.

186 *Compare* Manu, VIII, 351a.

259. Udyamya śastram āyāntam bhrūṇam apyātatāyinam
nihatya bhrūṇahā na syāt ahatvā bhrūṇahā bhavet.[187]
260. Apasarati yo yuddhāt jīvitārthī narādhamaḥ
jīvan eva mṛtaḥ sopi bhuṅkte rāṣṭrakṛtam tvagham.
261. Mitram vā svāminam tyaktvā nirgacchati raṇāt ca yaḥ
so'nte narakam āpnoti sa jīvan nindyate'khilaiḥ.
262. Mitram āpadgatam dṛṣṭvā sahāyam na karoti yaḥ
akīrtim labhate so'tra mṛto narakam ṛcchati.[188]
263. Visrambhāt śaraṇam prāptam śaktaḥ tyajati durmatiḥ
sa yāti narake ghore yāvat indrāścaturdaśa.

---

259. He who has raised a weapon against an approaching assassin, though this be a Vaidika Brahman, (and) killed him, should not be considered as a Vaidikabrahman-murderer ; if he has not killed him, he should be regarded as such.

Punishment of cowardice.

260. He who desirous of his life goes away from the battle is a very bad man, though alive he is surely dead ; he has to bear the sin done in the realm.

261. He who, having left his friend or his king, goes from the battle field, goes at his death to hell, and is blamed by all during his life.

262. He who, having seen his enemy going into danger, does not help him, acquires infamy here and goes, when dead, to hell.

263. The wicked, who though strong, deserts him who confidingly comes to him for protection, stays in a fearful hell, as long as there are fourteen Indras.

---

187 *See* Mahābhārata, Śāntiparva, Rājadharma, LVI, 28-30, and p. 38. *Compare* Manu, VIII, 350.
Gurum vā bālavṛddhau vā brāhmaṇam vā bahuśrutam
ātatāyinam āyāntam hanyāt evā vicārayan ;
and about *bhrūṇahā* Manu, VIII, 317.

188 *Compare* with this and the preceding Ślokas the Mahābhārata as above, 20-21.

264. Sudurvṛttam yadā kṣatram nāśayeyustu brāhmaṇāh yuddham kṛtvāpi śastrāstrairna tadā pāpabhāginaḥ.
265. Hīnam yadā kṣātrakulam nicairlokaḥ prapīḍyate tadāpi brāhmaṇā yuddhe nāśayeyuḥ tu tān dhruvam.
266. Uttamam māntrikāstreṇa nālikāstreṇa madhyamam śastraiḥ kaniṣṭham yuddham tu bāhuyuddham tato'dhamam.
267. Mantreritamahāśaktibāṇādyaiḥ śatrunāśanam māntrikāstreṇa tat yuddham sarvayuddhottamam smṛtam
268. Nālāgnicūrṇasaṁyogāt lakṣe golanipātanam nālikāstreṇa tat yuddham mahāhrāsakaram ripoḥ.
269. Kuntādiśastrasaṅghātairnāśanam ripūṇām ca yat śastrayuddham tu tat jñeyam nālāstrābhāvataḥ sadā.
270. Karṣaṇaiḥ sandhimarmāṇām pratilomānulomataḥ bandhanairghātanam śatroryuktyā tat bāhuyuddhakam.

---

264. If the Brahmans should even with arms and missiles destroy in a war bad behaving Kṣatriyas, they do then commit no sin.

265. If, when the Kṣatriya caste is weak, the world is oppressed by mean persons, then also should the Brahmans surely destroy those in war.

Modes of Fighting.

266. The best fight is with enchanted missiles, the middling is with tubular projectile weapons, the lowest with weapons, the worst is fighting with the arms.

267. The destruction of enemies by arrows and other weapons of great force and despatched by spells, and by enchanted missiles, is recorded as the best fighting of all.

268. The throwing of a ball by a tubular instrument through the application of gunpowder and a tube is very destructive to the enemy.

269. The destruction of the enemy which takes place by means of lances and other weapons, is always to be known as the combat with weapons in the absence of tubular projectile weapons.

270. The killing of the enemy by injuring his joints and vital

271. Nālāstrāṇi puraskṛtya laghūni ca mahānti ca
tat pṛṣṭhagāñśca pādātān gajāśvān pārśvayoḥ sthitān
kṛtvā yuddham prārabheta bhinnāmātyabalāriṇā
272. Sāmmukhyena prapātena pārśvābhyām apayānataḥ
yuddhānukūlabhūmestu yāvallābhastathāvidham.
273. Sainyārdhāṁśena prathamam senapairyuddham īritam
amātyagopitaiḥ paścāt amātyaiḥ saha tat bhavet,
nṛpasaṅgopitaiḥ paścāt svataḥ prāṇātyaye ca tat.
274. Dīrghadhvanipariśrāntam kṣutpipāsāhitaśramam[189]
vyādhidurbhikṣamaraṇaiḥ pīḍitam dasyuvidrutam ;[190]

---

parts, by tossing him backwards and forwards, and by grasping him, is properly regarded as the fighting with the arms of the body.

271. Having placed the small and big guns in front ; and behind them the infantry, and on the two flanks the elephants and horses, he should begin the battle, when the hostile army and ministers are disunited,

272. by attacking the enemy in front, by falling on him with the two wings, by retreating, in such a manner so far as the advantage of the ground favours the combat.

273. The battle should be first opened by generals with half the army, it should then be continued by the ministers with the troops under their command, and at last by the king himself with the troops under his special orders, when life at large is at stake.

274. If his own army is exhausted by a long march, experiences distress through hunger and thirst, is destroyed by disease, famine and death, is alarmed by marauders;

---

189 *See* Hitop., III, 108a.
Dīrghavartmapariśrāntam nadyadrivanasaṅkulam.

190 *See* Kāmand., XVIII, 50.
Dīrghe'dhvani pariśrāntam kṣutpipāsāhimaklamam
vyādhidurbhikṣamarakaiḥ pīḍanam dasyuvidrutam.
Hitop., III, 109a. Pramattam bhojanavyagram vyādhidurbhikṣapīḍitam

275. Paṅkapāṁsujalaskandhavyastam śvāsāturam tathā
prasuptam bhojane vyagram abhūmiṣṭham asaṁsthitam ;[191]
276. Ghorāgnibhayavitrastam vṛṣṭivātasamāhatam,[192]
evamādiṣu jātiṣu vyasaneṣu samākulam
svasainyam sādhu rakṣet tu, parasainyam vināśayet.[193]
277. Upāyān ṣaḍguṇān mantram śatroḥ svasyāpi cintayan
dharmayuddhaiḥ kūṭayuddhairhanyāt eva ripum sadā.
278. Yāne sapādabhṛtyā tu svabhṛtyān vardhayan nṛpaḥ
svadeham gopayan yuddhe carmaṇā kavacena ca ;

---

275. is troubled on the roads by much mud, dust and water, is also out of breath, is sleepy, is engaged in eating, has no proper place to stand upon, is in disorder ;

276. is frightened by the fear of horrible fires, is heavily exposed to wind and rain, and is distressed by such existing calamities, he should well guard it ; but he should destroy the army of his enemy, if it is in a similar state.

277. Considering the six-fold expedients and the design of his enemy and his own, he should surely always kill his enemy by fair and unfair fighting.

278. When the king gladdens his soldiers on the march with a quarter extra pay, protects his body in the battle with a shield and armour ;

---

[191] *See* Kāmandakīya, XVIII, 51b and 52a.
Paṅkapāṁśujalaklinnam vyastam puñjīkṛtam pathi
prasuptam bhojanavyagram abhūmiṣṭham asaṁsthitam.
Hitop., III, 109.
Pramattam bhojanavyagram vyādhidurbhikṣapīḍitam
asaṁsthitam abhūyiṣṭham vṛṣṭivātasamākulam.

[192] *See* Hitop., III, 108b. Ghorāgnibhayasantrastam kṣutpipāsārditam tathā, and Kāmandakīya, XVIII, 52b, Caurāgnibhayavitrastam vṛṣṭivātasamāhitam.

[193] *See* Kāmandakīya, XVIII, 53.
svasainyam sādhu rakṣeta parasainyam ca ghatayet.

279. Pāyayitvā madam saṁyak sainikān śauryavarddhanam
nālāstreṇa ca khaḍgādyaiḥ sainiko ghātayet arim.

280. Kuntena sādī bāṇena rathago gajago'pi ca
gajo gajena yātavyaḥ turageṇa turaṅgamaḥ.

281. Rathena ca ratho yojyaḥ pattinā pattir eva ca
ekenaikaśca śastreṇa śastram astreṇa vāstrakam.

282. Na ca hanyāt sthalārūḍham na klībam na kṛtāñjalim
na muktakeśam āsīnam na tavāsmīti vādinam.[194]

283. Na suptam na visannāham na nagnam na nirāyudham
na yudhyamānam paśyantam, yudhyamānam pareṇa ca.[195]

---

279. has made his soldiers drink up to a state of intoxication—the strengthener of bravery—; the soldier kills his enemy with a tubular instrument (*gun*), swords and other weapons.

280. A charioteer should be assailed by a lance, a person on a carriage or elephant by an arrow, an elephant by an elephant, a horse by a horse.

281. A carriage is to be opposed by a carriage, and a foot-soldier certainly by a foot-soldier, one person by another person, a weapon by a weapon, or a missile by a missile.

Who should not be killed.

282. He should not kill a person, who is alighted on the ground, nor one who is emasculated, nor one who has joined his hands as a supplicant, nor one who sits with dishevelled hair, nor one, who says, "I am thine;"

283. nor one who is asleep, nor one without a coat of mail, nor a naked, nor an unarmed person, nor a combatant who is looking on, nor one who is fighting with another;

---

[194] *See* Manu, VII, 91 ; Nītiprakāśikā, VII, 46 ; and Mahābhārata, Rāja-dharma, XCVI, 3, and XCVIII, 48a.

[195] *See* Manu, VII, 92.

na yudhyamānam paśyantam na pareṇa samāgatam ;
and Nītiprakāśikā, VII, 47.

284. Pibantam na ca bhuñjānam anyakāryākulam na ca
na bhītam na parāvṛttam satām dharmam anusmaran.[196]
285. Vṛddho bālo na hantavyo naiva strī kevalo nṛpaḥ,
yathāyogyam tu saṁyojya nighnan dharmo na hīyate.
286. Dharmayuddhe tu kūṭe vai na santi niyamā amī
na yuddham kūṭasadṛśam nāśanam balavadripoḥ.
287. Rāmakṛṣṇendrādidevaiḥ kūṭam evādṛtam purā ;
kūṭena nihato Bālir Yavano Namuciḥ tathā.
288. Praphullavadanenaiva tathā komalayā girā
kṣuradhāreṇa manasā ripoḥ chidram sulakṣayet.
289. Pañcāśītiśatānīkaḥ senākāryam vicintayan
sadaiva vyūhasaṅketavādyaśabdāntavartinaḥ
sañcareyuḥ sainikāśca rājarāṣṭrahitaiṣiṇaḥ.

---

284. nor one who is drinking or eating, nor one engaged in another matter, nor one who is frightened, nor one who is running away ; remembering the custom of the good.

285. Neither is an old man or a child to be killed, surely not a woman and especially not a king. If one kills, having fought in a suitable manner, no virtue is violated.

286. These restrictions exist in fair but not in unfair fighting, for the destruction of a powerful enemy there is no fighting like unfair fighting.

287. Unfair fighting was certainly observed by Rāma, Kṛṣṇa, Indra and other gods ; Bāli, Yavana and also Namuci were killed by unfair fighting.

288. With a cheerful face certainly and with a pleasing voice, but with a mind sharp as a razor he should always keep in view the vulnerable point of the enemy.

Rules how to drill an army.

289. A king with 8,500 soldiers should study the working of an army, and the soldiers should always march, being well acquainted with the words (of command), the bugle-calls, sounds, signs, and military arrays, wishing for the welfare of the king and kingdom.

---

[196] *See* Manu, VII, 93b.

290. Bheditām śatruṇā dṛṣṭvā svasenām ghātayet ca tām.
291. Pratyagre karmaṇi kṛte yodhairdadyāt dhanam ca tān
pāritoṣyam vādhikāram kramato' rham nṛpaḥ sadā.
292. Jalānnatṛṇasaṁrodhaiḥ śatrum sampīḍya yatnataḥ
purastāt viṣame deśe paścāt hanyāt tu vegavān.
293. Kūṭasvarṇamahādānairbhedayitvā dviṣadbalam
nityavisrambhasaṁsuptam prajāgarakṛtaśramam,
vilobhyāpi parānīkam apramatto vināśayet.
294. Kṣaṇam yuddhāya sajjeta kṣaṇam cāpasaret punaḥ
akasmāt nipatet dūrāt dasyuvat paritaḥ sadā.
295. Rūpyam hemaca kupyam ca yo yat jayati tasya tat[197]
dadyāt kāryānurūpam ca hṛṣṭo yodhān praharṣayan.

---

290. A king having observed that his army has been won over by the enemy, he should destroy it.

291. A king should always, after a fresh victory has been won by his soldiers, give them a gratifying reward, and deserving promotion in due order. *Rewards for soldiers.*

292. Having at first harassed the enemy in a hilly country by cutting off water, food and grass, he should afterwards vanquish him. *Harassing the enemy.*

293. Having sown dissensions in the hostile army by great gifts of counterfeit gold, and having deceived the (remaining) inimical host, which is sleeping in complete security and tired out by watches, a vigilant king should destroy it.

294. At one moment he should endeavour to fight, at another moment he should retreat again, he should suddenly fall upon him from far, being always on every side, like a robber.

295. The silver, gold and copper, which a soldier wins, belong to him, and the king should eagerly, gratifying the warriors, bestow on them rewards according to merit. *Concerning plunder.*

---

[197] *See* Manu, VII, 96.

296. Vijitya ca ripūn evam samādadyāt karam tathā
rājyāṁśam vā sarvarājyam nandayeta tataḥ prajāḥ.
297. Tūryamaṅgalaghoṣeṇa svakīyam puram āviśet
tatprajāḥ putravat sarvāḥ pālayetātmasātkṛtāḥ.
298. Niyojayet mantrigaṇam aparam mantracintane
deśe kāle ca pātre ca hyādimadhyāvasānataḥ
bhavet mantraphalam kīdṛk upāyena katham tviti.
299. Mantryādyadhikṛtaḥ kāryam yuvarājāya bodhayet
paścāt rājñe tu taiḥ sākam yuvarājo nivedayet.
300. Rājā saṁśāsayet ādau yuvarājam tataḥ tu saḥ
yuvarājo mantrigaṇān rājāgre te'dhikāriṇaḥ.
301. Sadasatkarma rājānam bodhayet hi purohitaḥ.

---

296. Having thus conquered his enemy he should take tribute, a part of the kingdom or the whole kingdom and gladden afterwards his subjects. Tribute.

297. He should enter his town amidst the propitious sound of musical instruments, and he should protect all the people confided to him like sons.

298. He should appoint one set of ministers (for administration); and another for the consideration of council, (to consider) according to place, time, and person, according to the beginning, midst or end, what means should be adopted and what would be the result of the policy. Administrative and executive officers.

299. The prime minister should inform the crown prince of the state of affairs, (and) the crown prince should together with these (ministers) afterwards impart it to the king. Privy council.

300. The king should at first issue instructions to the crown prince, the crown prince should then in the presence of the king give commands to the boards of ministers, and these to their officers.

301. The priest should truly teach the king right and wrong. Priest.

302. Grāmāt bahiḥ samīpe tu sainikān dhārayet sadā
grāmyasainikayorna syāt uttamarṇādharmarṇatā.

303. Sainikārtham tu paṇyāni sainye sandhārayet pṛthak
naikatra vāsayet sainyam vatsaram tu kadācana.

304. Senāsahasram sajjam syāt kṣaṇāt saṁśāsayet tathā
saṁśāsayet svaniyamān sainikān aṣṭame dine.

305. Caṇḍatvam ātatāyitvam rājakārye vilambanam
aniṣṭopekṣaṇam rājñah svadharmaparivarjanam,

306. Tyajantu sainikā nityam saṁlāpam apicāparaiḥ,
nṛpājñayā vinā grāmam na viśeyuḥ kadācana.

307. Svādhikāriganasyāpi hyaparādham diśantu naḥ,
mitrabhāvena vartadhvam svāmikārye sadākhilaiḥ.

---

302. The king should always place the soldiers outside the village but near; between villagers and soldiers there should be no relation of creditor and debtor. *Soldiers not to live in villages.*

303. He should open separately bazars in the camp for the sake of the soldiers, and he should never let an army remain at one place a year. *Bazaar.*

304. A king should order that a troop of a thousand men be ready at a moment's notice, he should teach the soldiers his orders in eight days.

305. "Let the soldiers always avoid committing a rash act, a murderous assault, delay in the service of the king, overlooking what is disagreeable to the king, and neglect in the performance of their duties; *General orders.*

306. "Let them avoid having conversations with strangers; nor should they enter a village without the permission of the king.

307. "Let them communicate to us any mistake made by an officer or a man belonging to the rank and file; and may you always be while in the service of the king in a state of friendship with all.

308. Sūjjvalānica rakṣantu śastrāstravasanāni ca
annam jalam prasthamātram pātram bahvannasādhakam.
309. Śāsanāt anyathā cārān vineṣyāmi yamālayam
bhedāyitā ripudhanam gṛhītvā darśayantu mām.
310. Sainikairabhyaset nityam vyūhādyanukṛtim nṛpaḥ
tathāyane'yane lakṣyam astrapātairbibhedayet.
311. Sāyam prātaḥ sainikānām kuryāt saṅgaṇanam nṛpaḥ
jātyākṛtivayodeśagrāmavāsān vimṛśya ca.
312. Kālam bhṛtyavadhim deyam dattam bhṛtyasya lekhayet
kati dattam hi bhṛtyebhyo vetane pāritoṣikam,
tat prāptipatram gṛhṇīyāt dadyāt vetanapatrakam.
313. Sainikāḥ śikṣitā ye ye teṣu pūrṇā bhṛtiḥ smṛtā
vyūhābhyāse niyuktā ye teṣvardhām bhṛtim āvahet.

---

308. "Let them keep very clean the arms, projectile weapons and dress, the food, water, the vessel which holds a *prastha*-measure and in which much food can be prepared.

309. "I shall remove the soldiers who disobey these orders to the abode of Death. The soldiers disbanded for plunder should show me what booty they have taken from the enemy."

310. A king should always practise with his soldiers the manner of formations, and other military drills, and should likewise try every half year to pierce the target by discharging projectile weapons.

311. A king should every evening and morning muster his soldiers, having enquired into their caste, physique, age, country, village and station. Muster.

312. He should write down the time, the amount of pay, what pay has been given and is to be given, what present has been given to the soldier in his pay. He should take a receipt for it, and should give a pay-bill. Pay.

313. For the soldiers, who are disciplined, is mentioned full-pay; to those, who are undergoing instruction in military formations he should give half-pay.

314. Asatkartrāśritam sainyam nāśayet śatruyogataḥ.

315. Nṛpasyāsadguṇaratāḥ ke guṇadveṣiṇo narāḥ
asadguṇodāsīnāḥ ke hanyāt tān vimṛśan nṛpaḥ,
sukhāsaktān tyajet bhṛtyān guṇinopi nṛpah sadā.

316. Susvāntalokaviśvastā yojyāḥ tvantaḥpurādiṣu
dhāryāḥ susvāntaviśvastā dhanādivyayakarmaṇi.

317. Tathā hi lokaviśvasto bāhyakṛtye niyujyate
anyathā yojitāḥ te tu parivādāya kevalaṁ.

318. Śatrusambandhino ye ye bhinnā mantrigaṇādayaḥ
nṛpadurguṇato nityam hṛtamānaguṇādikāḥ,
svakāryasādhakā ye tu subhṛtyā poṣayet ca tān.

---

314. A king should destroy an army which is attached to an untrustworthy general, who is in collusion with the enemy.

Treatment of servants.

315. A king, remembering those persons, who rejoice in his faults and hate his virtues, or who are indifferent to his faults, should kill them; servants who are devoted to pleasure he should dismiss, even if they are otherwise good.

Appointments how to be filled.

316. Well disposed and popular persons should be placed in his harem and elsewhere; well disposed and reliable persons should be employed in the distribution of money, &c.

317. A person who has gained the confidence of the people should be likewise appointed to posts outside the palace, otherwise if incompetent persons were appointed, they would only bring on discredit.

Creating dissensions in the enemy's camp.

318. He should support with good pay the group of ministers and other officers, who will serve his interests, and who while actually in the service of the enemy are disaffected, and who have lost their pride, virtue, and other good qualities through the badness of their king.

319. Lobhenā'sevanāt bhinnāḥ teṣvardhām bhṛtim āvahet
śatrutyaktān suguṇinah subhṛtyā pālayet nṛpaḥ.
320. Pararāṣṭre hṛte dadyāt bhṛtim bhinnāvadhim tathā
dadyāt ardhām tasya putre striyai pādamitām kila.
321. Hṛtarājyasya putrādau sadguṇe pādasammitam
dadyāt vā tadrājyatastu dvātṛṁśāṁśam prakalpayet.
322. Hṛtarājyasya nicitam kośam bhāgārtham āharet.
323. Kausīdam vā taddhanasya pūrvoktārdham prakalpayet,
taddhanam dviguṇam yāvat na tat tūrdhvam kadācana.
324. Svamahatvadyotanārtham hṛtarājyān pradhārayet
prāṅmānairyadi sadvṛttān durvṛttāstu prapīḍayet.

---

319. The king should give half pay to those who are gone away (and have come back) from greed and disregard; he should provide excellent persons who have left the enemy, with good pay.

320. If the kingdom of an enemy has been taken, he should give him pay from the time of the deposition; half the amount he should give to the son, a quarter surely to the wife.

What to give to a vanquished king.

321. He should give to the son or other relation of a dethroned prince, if he is very good, a fourth part of the income from the kingdom, or he may assign to him the thirty-second part of the kingdom.

322. He should take for his own share the amassed treasure of the dethroned prince.

323. Or he may fix on the dethroned prince the interest accruing from the treasure, *i.e.*, the above mentioned portion ($\frac{1}{32}$), till the total sum (received by him) is double the amount of the treasure.

324. He should maintain well the dethroned princes for the glory of his own greatness, if they are good with the honors formerly enjoyed by them; but if bad, he should suppress them.

325. Aṣṭadhā daśadhā vāpi kuryāt dvādaśadhāpi vā
yāmikārtham ahorātram yāmikān vīkṣya nānyathā.

326. Ādau prakalpitān aṁśān bhajeyuryāmikāstathā
ādyaḥ punastvantimāṁśam svapūrvāṁśam tato'pare.

327. Punarvā yojayet tadvat ādye'ntyam cāntime tataḥ
svapūrvāṁśam dvitīye'hni dvitīyādiḥ kramāgatam.

328. Caturbhyastvadhikān nityam yāmikān yojayet dine
yugapad yojayet dṛṣṭvā bahūn vā kāryagauravam.

329. Caturūnān yāmikānstu kadā naiva niyojayet.

330. Yadrakṣyam upadeśyam yat ādeśyam yāmikāya tat
tatsamakṣam hi sarvam syāt yāmiko'pica tat tathā.

Watchmen.

325. For the sake of the watchmen he should divide night and day into eight, ten or twelve watches, having previously looked at the (the number of the) watchmen, not otherwise.

326. The watchmen will also share (amongst them all) the originally fixed watches; the first watchman will again take the last watch, and each of the others will take the watch of his predecessor.

327. Or he may also appoint as before the last watchman to the first and last watch; the second watchman and the others should in due order obtain on the second day, &c. the watch of the first watchman.

328. He should always appoint every day more than four watchmen, or on some occasions having seen that the work is heavy, he should appoint many.

329. He should never appoint less than four watchmen.

330. The watchman should be told what is to be guarded, and what is to be communicated; all should be before his eyes, and the watchman should do it accordingly.

331. Kīlakoṣṭe tu svarṇādi rakṣet niyamitāvadhi
svāṁśānte darśayet anyayāmikam tu yathārthakam.

332. Kṣaṇe kṣaṇe yāmikānām kāryam dūrāt subodhanam.

333. Satkṛtān niyamān sarvān yadā sampādayet nṛpaḥ
tadaiva nṛpatiḥ pūjyo bhavet sarveṣu nānyathā.

334. Yasyāsti niyatam karma niyataḥ sadgraho yadi
niyato'sadgrahatyāgo nṛpatvam so'śnute ciram.

335. Yasyāniyamitam karma sādhutvam vacanam tvapi
sadaiva kuṭilaḥ syāt tu svapadāt drāk vinaśyati.

336. Nāpi vyāghragajāḥ śaktā mṛgendram śāsitum yathā
na tathā mantriṇaḥ sarve nṛpam svacchandagāminam.

---

331. He should up to the appointed time guard the gold and other things in the bolted treasury, (and) at the end of his watch he should show the amount of the treasure to another watchman.

332. There should be kept continually from a distance a good lookout on the watchmen.

Respect enjoyed by a king.

333. If a king should succeed in having all his orders well executed, he will surely be honoured among all men, but not otherwise.

334. The king, who is steady at his work, shows kindness to good people and discountenances bad persons, enjoys his kingdom for a long time.

335. The king, who is unsteady in his work, good behaviour and speech, and who is always deceitful, disappears soon from his throne.

336. As tigers and elephants even are not able to govern the lion, thus also all ministers are not able to govern a king, who goes on as he likes.

337. Nibhṛtā dhikṛtāstena nissāratvam hi teṣvataḥ
gajo nibadhyate naiva tūlabhārasahasrakaiḥ.
338. Uddhartum drāk gajaḥ śaktaḥ paṅkalagnagajam balī,
nītibhraṣṭanṛpam tvanyanṛpa uddhāraṇakṣamaḥ.
339. Balavannṛpabhṛtye' lpe' pi śrīḥ tejo yathā bhavet
na tathā hīnanṛpatau tanmantriṣvapi no tathā.
340. Bahūnām aikamatyam hi nṛpaterbalavattaram
bahusūtrakṛto rajjuḥ siṁhādyākarṣaṇakṣamaḥ.
341. Hīnarājyo ripubhṛtyo na sainyam dhārayet bahu,
kośavṛddhim sadā kuryāt svaputrādyabhivṛddhaye.
342. Kṣudhayā nidrayā sarvam aśanam śayanam śubham
bhavet yathā tathā kuryāt anyathāśu daridrakṛt.

---

337. By the king are humbled and censured the ministers, among them is therefore surely weakness ; an elephant is not bound even by 1,000 loads of cotton.

338. A strong elephant is able to draw out quickly another elephant who sticks in the mud ; a king is only able to reform an iniquitous king.

339. Even if the servants of a mighty king are insignificant there may be power and splendour ; but it will not be the same with a weak king, even if his ministers are not so.

340. The unanimity of many makes a king very strong ; a rope made of many strings is able to drag a lion and other beasts.

341. A king whose kingdom is reduced and who has become a dependent of his enemy should not maintain a large army, he should always increase his treasure, for the recovery of power by his son and descendants.

A weak kingdom how to strengthen

342. He should so work that through hunger and sleepiness every kind of food and couch becomes agreeable, otherwise he will soon become poor.

343. Diśānayā vyayam kuryāt nṛpo nityam na cānyathā.
344. Dharmanītivihīnā ye durbalā api vai nṛpāḥ,
sudharmabalayugrājñā daṇḍyāste cauravat sadā.
345. Sarvadharmāvanāt nīcanṛpo'pi śreṣṭhatām iyāt
uttamo'pi nṛpo dharmanāśanāt nīcatām iyāt.
346. Dharmādharmapravṛttau tu nṛpa eva hi kāraṇam
sa hi śreṣṭhatamo loke nṛpatvam yaḥ samāpnuyāt.
347. Manvādyairādṛto yo'rthaḥ tadartho Bhārgaveṇa vai,
dvāviṁśatiśatam ślokā nītisāre prakīrtitāḥ.
348. Śukroktanītisāram yaḥ cintayet aniśam sadā
vyavahāradhuram voḍhum sa śakto nṛpatirbhavet.
349. Na kaveḥ sadṛśī nītiḥ triṣu lokeṣu vidyate
kāvyaiva nītiranyā tu kunītirvyavahāriṇām.

---

343. A king should always spend in this manner, not otherwise.

344. Those kings who are surely deficient in righteousness and good behaviour, and are also weak, should be punished by a strong and righteous king, like thieves.

345. A lowbred king even may obtain excellence by the protection of righteousness, while a king of the highest caste may be ruined through the suppression of righteousness.

346. A king is surely the cause for the prevalence of right and wrong; he who obtains kingship is surely the very best in the world.

347. This matter concerning worldly prosperity which was respected by Manu and others was also surely respected by Bhārgava; 2,200 double verses are told in his essence of polity.

Excellence of Śukra's polity.

348. He who would always consider the essence of polity spoken by Śukra, may become a king capable of bearing the burden of administration.

349. Such a polity as that of the Poet (Śukra) is not known in the three worlds. The Polity (propounded) by the Poet is (good) polity, any other polity among men is bad policy.

350. Nāśrayanti ca ye nītim mandabhāgyāstu te nṛpāḥ,
kātaryāt dhanalobhāt vā syurvai narakabhājanāḥ.

---

350. Those unfortunate princes, who out of cowardice or cupidity do not have recourse to this polity, will surely have their share in Hell.

SCHEME OF TRANSLITERATION.

	Consonants.	Vowels.	Diphthongs.
Gutturals	k kh g gh ṅ h ḥ	a ā	e ai
Palatals	c ch j jh ñ y ś	i ī	
Linguals	ṭ ṭh ḍ ḍh ṇ r ṣ	ṛ ṝ	
Dentals	t th d dh n l s	ḷ	
Labials	p ph b bh m v ḥ	u ū	o au

Anusvāra .. .. .. ṁ (*real*), ṃ (*unreal*) ; Avagraha ʼ.

APPENDIX.

IDENTIFICATION OF THE MANIPURA OF THE MAHĀBHĀRATA WITH MANIPURA OR MANALŪRU OR MADURA IN SOUTH INDIA.

On a previous occasion (pp. 66 and 67) we mentioned the city of Maṇipura as a place to which the Mahābhārata according to Mr. Talboys Wheeler ascribes fortifications provided with firearms.

This Maṇipura is declared by Mr. Wheeler to be the modern "Munnipur in the extreme east beyond the Bengal frontier . . . a secluded valley lying between Eastern Bengal and Burmah; and the people appear to be a genuine relic of the ancient Nāgas."[199]

The late Professor Christian Lassen, by far the greatest authority on matters connected with Indian Archæology, inclines to place it on the Eastern Coast of India south of Chicacole at the mouth of the *Lāṅgulya* river, identifying it with a locality he calls Manphur-Bunder.[200]

In order to fix the locality of Maṇipura it is necessary to follow Arjuna on his journey as described in the first book of the Mahābhārata.[201] Arjuna goes first to the North, reaches the Ganges, bathes in the holy river, and meets here the fair Ulūpī, with whom he stays for some time. He visits all the holy places in Aṅga, Vaṅga, and Kaliṅga. Pursuing his road to the South along the Mahendra mountains, he crosses Kaliṅga, goes along the coast and reaches Maṇipura. Here

---

199 *See* History of India, I, 144, 149, 421 and elsewhere.

200 *See* Indische Alterthumskunde, I, 676, 677, (563). 2nd Note "der Name scheint im Manphur-Bunder, erhalten zu sein, welches bei Cikakul nahe bei Koringapaṭam liegt."

201 *See* Mahābhārata, Ādiparva, Chap. 174, 176; Bhāratacampū, III. Stavaka; Oriental Hist. MSS. Vol. I, 225, 226.

reigned the king Citravāhana, who had an only daughter Citrāṅgadā. Arjuna demanded her in marriage, after having made himself known. The king did not object to this request, but demanded that, as Citrāṅgadā was his only child, —for no Rāja of Maṇipura had ever had or would have more than one child,—the son born to Arjuna by his daughter should become king of Maṇipura. To this Arjuna consented and a son, Babhruvāhana, was born to Citrāṅgadā, and after Arjuna had staid for three years in Maṇipura, he left it, turned towards the Western Coast, wandered along it to Gokarṇa, and finally met Kṛṣṇa at Dvārakā. In the horse sacrifice Arjuna came once more to Maṇipura, fought with, and was killed by, his son Babhruvāhana, but was revived through the life-restoring jewel.

Deciding on the evidence before us as taken from the Mahābhārata, Mr. Wheeler's identification of the ancient Maṇipura with the modern Munnipur falls to the ground, and with it all his explanations of the significance of this myth. That the stories concerning Arjuna's journey to Maṇipura should be known among the Munnipurees of our days, and that they should claim to be the descendants of the inhabitants of ancient Maṇipura[202] need not astonish anybody. By this time the contents of the Mahābhārata are pretty well known all over India and its bordering states, and the Munnipurees do not stand alone in arrogating to themselves historical fame by taking advantage of the resemblance of names. There exist in India many places called Maṇipura.

Equally wrong, though less objectionable, is the conjecture of Lassen. There does not exist near Chicacole a place called Manphur-Bunder. The name of the town he thought of is not Manphur-Bunder, but Mafūs-Bandar. It lies on the left bank of the Lāṅgulya river near the sea, and is a comparatively modern place, as its name, which is a mixture

---

[202] *See* History of India, I. p. 149.

of Arabic and Persian words, clearly indicates. Māfūs Bandar (మాఫూసుబందరు) should be properly transcribed *Maḥfūz Bandar* (محفوظ بندر), which means a *secure harbour*, serving once probably Chicacole (*Śrīkākulam*) for such a purpose. Professor Lassen anxious to find a place on the north-eastern coast of the Dekkan which he could identify with Maṇipura, the capital of Babhruvāhana, fixed on Mafūs Bandar, mistaking *Mafūs* for *Manphur* (Maṇipura) most likely in consequence of a wrong application of the diacritical points over two letters. It may here be remarked that the originally Persian word *Bandar* is quite commonly used in Telugu, in the meaning of *harbour*, thus, *e.g.*, Masulipatam is generally called Bandar. The reason of this fact is that the seafaring population are mostly Muhammedans, the Arabs being in former times great navigators in these parts of the world.[203]

I believe that Professor Lassen was to a great extent induced to fix Maṇipura so far north, by limiting too much the extent of the Mahendra-mountain range, which he opined to be a particular mountain situated in Kaliṅga, and starting from these premises he went so far as to declare that the country Kaliṅga was wrongly mentioned in the Mahābhārata, as the region which, together with Aṅga and Vaṅga, Arjuna has passed through on his journey. The name Mahendra can apply to all the mountains near the Eastern Coast, including the Eastern Ghāṭs as well as the mountains near the sea of Bengal in the utmost south. Indra is the regent of the East, and the whole Eastern Coast is under his protection; a mountain near Rājamandry in the north is called *Rājamahēndra* and the highest and most southern mountain in India bears the name *Mahendragiri.*

In the Rāmāyaṇa Hanumān is said to have jumped from

---

[203] North of Vizianagram lies inland a place called Muṇipurīpēṭa.

the Mahendra mountain to Ceylon (Laṅkā). This exploit would have been somewhat more difficult if Hanumān had to jump from Mafūsbandar to that island; as he would have been obliged to leap into the dark, for he could hardly see Ceylon from a place near Chicacole[204].

The mountain from which Hanumān is said to have jumped to Ceylon, bears to this day the name *Mahendragiri*. It is the same hill, near which the fierce warrior sage Paraśurāma lived. This Mahendragiri is the highest and most prominent peak north of Cape Comorin. It is 5,430 feet high and serves the sailors as a land mark; on its southern side lies the town Pannaguḍi.

On the east of the south part of the Eastern Ghāṭs, which is called there by the inhabitants also Mahendra, lies Madura, and a few miles still further east lies Maṇalūru. It may be here remarked, that Maṇalūru or Maṇipura lay formerly much nearer to the sea, as India has increased considerably on this side of the coast. In old legends we read, that the sea encroached on some occasions to the walls of Madura.

The Sanskrit name of this Maṇalūru is Maṇipura, and as such it was the capital of the ancient Pāṇḍya kingdom. Kulaśekhara Pāṇḍya is mentioned both in Tamil and Telugu records as the founder of Maṇipura, which was otherwise known by the name of Maṇalūru. The local traditions all coincide on this point. Maṇipura or Maṇalūru was the original site of the capital of the Pāṇḍya kings, which was afterwards transferred to Madura in its immediate neigh-

[204] *See* Rāmāyaṇa Kiṣkindhākāṇḍa, LXVII, 40—43.

40. Āruroha nagaśreṣṭham mahendram arimardanaḥ.

43. Vicacāra hariśreṣṭho mahendrasamavikramaḥ.

Ibidem, Sundarakāṇḍa, I, 15, 213, 214.

Rāmāyaṇasaṅgraha, Sundarakāṇḍa, I, 1.

1. Tato Mahendraśikharāt utplutya Hanumān balī surasāsiṁhike bhittvā Laṅkābahiravātarat.

Mahānāṭaka, Sundarakāṇḍa, I, 14, 15, 126, 127.

bourhood.[205] In some chronicles Maṇipura is also called Kalyāṇapura; the proposed identification of Kalyāṇapura with Kurkhi is quite without foundation.

Occasional excavations round Maṇalūru have brought to light substantial evidences of ancient structures, especially in the fields of Maṇalūru Cintāmaṇi, midway between the present Maṇalūru and Madura; old coins and ancient gold ornaments have also been found there in quantities. The neighbouring country round Maṇalūru stands among the natives in the reputation of containing many hidden treasures, and people often try to find them by means of the wand.

It is a most important coincidence that in some old MSS. of the Mahābhārata, instead of the name Maṇipura, the chapters of the Aśvamedha, which should contain it, give actually the name Maṇalūru.[206]

In the "Oriental Historical Manuscripts" of the Rev. Mr. Taylor occurs, instead of Maṇalūru the name Manavūru, but from further evidence given by Mr. Taylor himself, both names apply to one and the same place.[207] In some chronicles Madura is substituted for Maṇipura, and Arjuna is said to have married the daughter of the Pāṇḍya king of Madura.[208]

---

205 *See* Tamil Kadjān MS. No. 2327 in the Government Orient. MSS. Library ibidem, Local Records XLVII, 105: "Madhurasamīpamandunna Maṇipuram anagā Maṇalūru candravaṁśam Kulaśekharapāṇḍyuḍu rājyaparipālana, saṁv. 4,100." According to some Kulaśekhara himself transferred the capital from Maṇipura to Madura.

206 *See* Aśvamedha, LXI, 1—3; LXVII, 1; LXVIII, 1; LXIX, 1.

LXI. 1. Krameṇa saha yastvevam vicaran Bharatarṣabha
*Maṇalūru*paterdeśam upāyāt saha Pāṇḍavaiḥ.
2. Śrutvā tu nṛpatirvīram pitaram Babhruvāhanaḥ
niryayau vinayenāryo brāhmaṇārghyapurassaraḥ.
3. *Maṇalūre*śvaram caivam upāyāntam dhanañjayaḥ.

LXVII. 1. Putrastasya mahābhāgo *Maṇalūre*śvaro yuvā.

LXVIII. 1. Prāyopaviṣṭe nṛpatau *Maṇalūre*śvare tathā.

LXIX. 1. Kim āgamanakṛtyam te Kauravyakulanandinī
*Maṇalūru*patestasya tathaiva caraṇājire.

207 *See* Oriental Historical Manuscripts, by William Taylor, Missionary, I, 13, 57, 120.

208 *See* Ibidem, p. 122.

The adventures of Arjuna during his exile have always been a subject of great interest among the Indians, and many of his exploits have gained for him a favorite place among the Pāṇḍava heroes.

Especially his journey to Maṇipura has been largely commented upon, as through his stay at that place and his marriage with the crown-princess Citrāṅgadā, the family of the Pāṇḍyas became united with that of the Pāṇḍavas.

Citravāhana and his grandson Babhruvāhana are frequently mentioned as Pāṇḍyas as well in old as in more modern records, and on this point they are unanimous. Mr. Nelson, the able compiler of the Manual of the Madura District, is by far too positive, when he says that in the Mahābhārata no mention is made of Arjuna having married a Pāṇḍya princess; for there exist copies which contain such an account.[209]

The fame and power of the Pāṇḍavas must have spread all over India and beyond it, for the conqueror of Ceylon, Vijaya, belongs also to this family.

Whether the connection of the Pāṇḍyas with the Pāṇḍavas was a real one, or whether it was only assumed by the former to invest themselves with greater authority and to raise their position in the eyes of the people is now difficult to find out, but the belief in such connection is a matter of fact.

According to a chronicle quoted by Mr. Taylor the Pāṇḍya kings were descended from Yayāti, the son of Nahuṣa. Yayāti had two sons by Devayānī, the daughter of Uśanas, Yadu and Turvaśa (Turvasu). "The younger brother of Yadu (*i.e.*, Turvaśa,) was the first Pandian. The place of his reigning was Manalūr. Among those of this race, one, named Kulaśeghara Pandian, by the favor of Śiva, cut down a forest of Kadambu trees, and built a town called Madura, where he lived."[210]

---

[209] *See* Manual of the Madura District, by J. H. Nelson, M.A., III, 49.

[210] *See* Oriental Historical Manuscripts, I, 120.

We thus see, if the legend just narrated rests on any authority, that Maṇipura or Maṇalūru through its king, who was a son of daughter of Śukra, is connected with Śukrācārya,—the presumed author of the Śukranīti, and the expounder of the fabrication of gunpowder and the construction and handling of guns,—is the same Maṇipura, of which we have read in the Mahābhārata, that it was provided with firearms and guns against the attack of its enemies. If Maṇipura is the place which corresponds to the site of Maṇipura (Maṇalūru) near Madura, a great many otherwise inexplicable contradictions are easily solved.

The affection with which the Pāṇḍavas are remembered in India, and especially in the South, seems to me not only due to the interest which the story of their sufferings, their bravery, and final victory excited everywhere, but also to some cause by which their memory was effectually kept alive.

There are no monuments of great antiquity in Southern India, especially on the Eastern Coast, with which legendary lore does not somehow connect the name of the Pāṇḍavas. Thus we observe that their name is associated with the rock-cut caves in Māmaṇḍūr near Conjeveram, and the same occurs in many other places, perhaps also at the rock temples of Kalugumalai.

The famous Seven Pagodas near Madras, whose carvings are celebrated all over India, do not form an exception to this rule. The monoliths representing rathas (cars) or shrines named after Dharmarāja, Bhīma, Arjuna, Nakula and Sahadeva, and even to Draupadī, are among the most ancient of the carvings. Arjuna especially is a favorite; there are two rathas named after him, though one of them contains now an image of Gaṇeśa, and the most splendid carving, of which there exist also two copies, though one is in an incomplete state, is called Arjuna's penance. We must not forget that Arjuna is the presumed ancestor of the Pāṇḍyas.

I believe that these and other such carvings originated with the Pāṇḍya princes, who, by honoring their ancestors, conferred still greater distinction on themselves. A reigning dynasty alone could have undertaken the construction of such works. The assumption that these carvings originated with the Pāṇḍyas, under whose sway for some time the whole Eastern Coast remained, does not contradict any historical statement, especially as the reign of the Pāṇḍya kings extended over a long period.

The execution of these sculptures is generally ascribed to the architectural energy of Buddhists and Jains, but there is nothing against the assumption that the Pāṇḍyas may have once also followed the religious tenets of the Buddhists and Jains and supported their co-religionists in the same manner in the South as the Maurya Kings of Pāṭaliputra did in the North.

If this hypothesis can be proved to rest on historical evidence, we shall perhaps be able to settle before long the date of the construction of these rock carvings in a more satisfactory manner than has been done up to this day.

INDEX.

The figures refer to the pages.

A.

B.

Bālakāṇḍa, 25, 29.
Bāli, 72, 133.
Balls of guns, 65, 107, 108.
Bamboo guns, 66.
Bān, 71.
Bāṇa, 71.
Bāṇapetra, Bāṇapaṭṭrai, 71.
Bandar, 147.
Baṅga *see* Vaṅga.
Bārhaspatya, 35.
Battering ram, 22.
Battle axe, 10, 21, 108.
Bavaria, 50.
Baza, siege of, 49.
Bazaar, 136.
Beam, 22.
Beckmann, Johann, 47, 48, 59, 60.
Bellay, Martin, 50.
Bengal, 60, 145.
Bengāli, 62.
Bhadra elephant, 88, 89.
Bharadvājā, 37, 75, 76.
Bhāradvāja, 36.
Bhāratacampū, 67, 145.
Bhārgava, 34, 37, 76.
Bhatnīr, 51.
Bhīma, 151.
Bhogavyūha, 6.
Bhṛgu, 34.
Bhṛsuṇḍi, 16.
Bhrūṇa, Bhrūṇahā, 38, 128.
Bible, 58.
Bohlen, P. von, 68.
Bontajammuḍu, 62.
Böthlingk, 69.
Bow, 11, 12, 108.
Brahma, 9, 23, 25, 35, 36, 76, 125.
———'s daṇḍanīti, 35.
Brahman, 2, 31, 37, 38, 43, 64, 75, 124, 125, 127, 128.
———, self-estimation of a, 2; Brahman murder when condonable, 127, 128.
Brahmanic community, 72.
Brahmaśīrṣa, 26, 30.
Brahmāstra, 30.
Breechloader, 50.
Breisgau, 45.
Bṛhaspati, 34, 35, 36, 40.
Bridle, 101, 102.
Broadsword, 109
Brunswickers, 50.
Buddhist, 152.
Bull, 6; age of a, 99; teeth of a, 101.
Bullrings, 102.
Bumarang, 18, 19.
Burmah, 66, 145.
Byzantine princess, 47.

C.

Cakra, 10, 15.
Cakravartī, 94.
Calatropis gigantea, 61, 62, 106, 107.
Calicut, 76.
Caligula, 53.
Camel, 6, 98, 99; age of a, 101.
Camphor, 63, 107.
Camū, 4, 5.
Cāṇakya, 37.
Caṇḍāla, 33.
Cannon, 49.
Caracalla, 53.
Carriage, 88.
Caspian Sea, 47.
Castanheda, 76.
Ceylon, 147, 148, 150.
Chand, 52.
Charcoal, 56, 61, 62, 63, 64, 106, 107.
Chariot, 5, 6, 88.
Charles V, 49.
Chicacole, 145, 146, 147, 148.
China, 45, 47.
Chinese, 45, 51, 52;—cracker, 65.
Christ Church, Oxford, 49.
Cintāmaṇi, 94.
Citrāṅgadā, 146, 150.
Citravāhana, 146, 150.
Clavigo, Gongalez, 51.
Clement IV, 46.
Club, 13 (crooked), 14, 16 (octagon-headed), 20, 108.
Code of Gentoo Laws, 69, 70.
Codification of the law, 74.
Coimbatore, 78.
Coins, value of, 86.
Cola, 33.
Comorin, Cape, 148.
Constantinople, 47.
Cow commits Brahman murder, 24.
Cowardice punished, 128.
Cowhornspear, 17.
Creci, 49.
Crocodile, 57.
Cronstedt, A. F. von., 59.
Cullakī (culukī, culumpī), 56, 57, 58.
Culuka, 56.
Cūrṇa, 64.
Curtius, Quintus, 69.
Cyavana, 75.

D.

Dadhīci, 16, 17, 23, 24.
Dagger, 21.
Daibal, 53.
Daitya, 28, 34.

E.

F.

G.

H.

I.

J.

K.

Manjanīk, 53.
Manmatha, 67, 68.
Manœuvring position, 111, 112.
Manphur Bander, 145, 146, 147.
Mantra of the Dhanurveda, 10.
Mantramukta, 10, 30.
Manu, 12, 18, 25, 36, 37, 40, 43, 70, 71, 73, 81, 118, 124–27, 132, 133, 134, 143.
Marcasite, 50.
Marching, 113, 116, 117, 119.
Marcus Graecus, 46, 47.
Mardita, 65.
Marīci, 25.
Marīcipatala, 79.
Maruna, 64.
Marundu, 64.
Match, lighted, 50.
Mathana, 27.
Māṣa, 86.
Masulipatam, 147.
Maurya kings, 152.
Mausala, 27.
Mausalāstra, 29.
Mauṣṭika, 21.
Mavellaka, 33.
Māyāstra, 27.
Mayukhī, 22.
Medhya, 97.
Medinīkara, 57.
Man, age of, 98, 99.
Mesopotamia, 47.
Ministers, number of, 40.
Miśra elephant, 88, 89.
Missiles, 105.
Mleccha, 33.
Mode of fighting, 129, 130.
Mogols, 52 ; history of the, 3 ; empire of the, 51.
Moha, 29.
Mokatta of Velletri, 50.
Moors, 46.
Mouchet, 50.
Mṛga elephant, 88, 89, 90.
Mudar, 62.
Mudgara, 20.
Muhammed Kazim, 53.
Muhammedans, 78, 147.
Mujmalut Tavarikh, 64.
Mukta, 10.
Muktāmukta, 10, 25, 29.
Muktasandhārita, 11.
Mulfūzāt i Timuri, 51.
Muster, 137.
Musala, 21.
Musalī, 57.
Musket, 14, 50.
Musuṇḍi, 16.

N.

Nābhaka, 28.
Naḍa, nāḍi, nāḍī, 60.
Nāḍika, 66, 68, 69.
Nagāstra, 27.
Nairāśya, 28.
Naiṣadha, 14, 67, 68, 81.
Nāla (nala), 66.
Nālika (nalika, nālīka), 14, 66, 68, 71.
Names of princes according to their income, 87, 88.
Namuci, 72, 133.
Nānārtharatnamālā, 38.
Nandanāstra, 27.
Napoleon the Great, 148.
Narashy, 62.
Nārāyaṇāstra, 30.
Natron, 58, 59.
Needle gun, 50.
Nelson, J. H., 150.
Neter, 58.
Netherlands, 50.
Nickel, 59.
Nicholas III, 46.
Niṣka, 7, 86.
Nistriṁśā, 25.
Nītiprakāśikā, 3-26, 30, 31, 32, 36, 66, 68, 71, 73, 74, 80, 81, 132.
Nītisāra, 34, 35.
Nītiśāstra, 4, 68.
Nitrum, 58, 59.
North-India, 47.
Nürnberg, 50.

O.

Officers, administrative and executive, 136.
Oil, 32 (boiling and explosive), 55 taken from a big worm (crocodile), 57.
Oilsprings, 47.
Opiment, 63, 107.
Orders, general military, 136, 137.
Ou, king of, 52.
Oxford, 45, 49.
Oxydracae, 53.

P.

Padma, 93.
Padmavyūha, 93.
Pahlava, 33.
Paila, 4.

Q.

R.

S.

Y.

For EU product safety concerns, contact us at Calle de José Abascal, 56–1°,
28003 Madrid, Spain or eugpsr@cambridge.org.

www.ingramcontent.com/pod-product-compliance
Ingram Content Group UK Ltd.
Pitfield, Milton Keynes, MK11 3LW, UK
UKHW012341130625
459647UK00009B/457

* 9 7 8 1 1 0 8 0 8 0 3 9 2 *